PASSWORDS

FINDING THE MISSING LINK TO THE DESIRED PLACE

FAVOR E. ALANWOKO

Teresa Skinner
Publishers

Copyright © 2014 by Favor E. Alanwoko
ISBN: 978-0-9755202-8-4
2nd Edition

All rights reserved.
No part of this book may be reproduced in any form or by any electronic or mechanical means, including information storage and retrieval systems, without written permission from the author, except for the use of brief quotations in a book review.

For everyone on a search... Matthew 13:45

CONTENTS

Preface   vii
Introduction   ix

Key 1 - Personality   1
Key 2 - Purpose   13
Key 3 - Parents   21
Key 4 - Priorities   27
Key 5 - Peace   41
Key 6 - Plan   49
Key 7 - Process   63
Key 8 - Practice   73
Key 9 - The Secret 'P'   77

About the Author   85

PREFACE

Few months to the completion of this work, I was walking with a couple of friends and I commented on my upcoming book. One of them humorously asked me if it is a fictional book. I replied, no! I didn't quite get why he would choose to think I'll write a fictional book, so I asked him why? He reminisces on our high school days and one of the adventure books I wrote at the time. What he did not remember, I think, is how I didn't finish the book not to talk of making a move to publish it, because I couldn't continue the story. However, with the discovery of *Passwords*, came an amazing weight of inspiration. The intestinal fortitude to birth this work just didn't cease to flow through.

    I started writing this book with what I would like to call my basic 'Ps'. I had taught people that there are three basic 'Ps', namely; People, Place and Plan. The onion of this teaching was that if you had positive relationships and are placed in the right location, with the right plan, you will in no doubt be a success. However, as I proceeded with the work, I made other interesting discoveries that further embellished this work. The interesting thing about this book, I think, is the arrangement; how it relates to some 'unpopular' parts of the subject of success. The principles of success are no secrets. They are rather too obvious and somehow, very simple; so, by reason of familiarity with them, most people don't really take them into serious considerations. So, while they could be common, they are yet unpopular.

I try to present this my somewhat unconventional view of success, in a direct and simple manner – easy to read and understand. I feel more comfortable avoiding the grammatical complications that could impinge clear understanding of this book especially by young minds. The illustrations and events in this book are personal. I tried to use only examples that refer to me and keep the identities of any secondary personality discreet. The personal events in this book are presented without sentiments to relate with the simplicity of success. This book is designed to be concise and compact. It is the sort of book you could carry around and even get to memorize. If I was to go by another name, I would gladly title this book, 'Put that 'P' in Place'. But, that now, is my advice to you as you read through the pages of the book.

Special thanks to my parents, Dr. and Pst. Mrs. Sylvester C. Alanwoko for their huge support and encouragement. To Rev. Gordon and Teresa Skinner, directors at All Nations International, thanks for being a shoulder of support. Pst. Florence Akujobi (Mommy), Pst. Gail Adamoschek, Sarah Falcone, Ugwumsinachi Osondu, Chidera Akujobi, and all those who were there from the first edition, Thank you!

INTRODUCTION

If you knew the one thing you'll have to do to get to where you wish, what do you think it could be? Let me rephrase that. What is the missing link between your desire and your reality? Have you ever felt like you are missing it? That is, you get this feeling of something not in place, like something is missing as you pursue a beautiful and fulfilling life for yourself. This somewhat discreet ingredient to success may to some extent explain why many believe that success is a discovery – your ability to discover and identify the appropriate piece to fit into your puzzle board. Imagine if you knew the exact pieces to put into your life's success puzzle. Then I could be writing a book about you because no doubt, you will be a success.

A lady once sat for an examination in which she was to fill in the missing word in a statement. She read and peered through the statement over and over and it just seemed, perfect! No trace of any word missing. So, she was put off at whatever it was the lecturer was thinking and wondered if he was aware of the 'correctness' of the statement. So, she almost left the question as a question having the answer in itself. Suddenly, like light flashing through her eyes, she spots a missing word. Eureka! Guess what it was? It was the letter A - the indefinite article? 'Wow!' She thought, 'so intricate.' How could she have ever noticed? You see, to succeed, you must take into account necessary details. Look to see, listen to hear!

One of the finest tricks used in puzzle games, is to put the missing item right in front of you yet what you are looking at seems too common to house what you are looking for. Perhaps, success' finest principles revolve around the letter 'P'. It is like one of those puzzle tricks which this book clearly tries to fix.

Success is attained by following the basic principles which in most cases are simple. In *Passwords* I try to solve the puzzle of most success patterns and success stories. A systematic application of the principles hacked in this book will turn you into the dream success you wish. It is that simple! But you need to commit to the process. Oops! Notice principles, process… well, now you see what I'm saying. The letter 'P' has something big to say about success.

Let me further digest this for you. When a woman is to be delivered of a baby what command is issued to her…, sorry, screamed at her? Is it 'Woman, put yourself together? Or 'What did you eat on your way to this place?' Nope. It is simply but frantically, "Pushhhhhh!!!" To some this may not seem like much, only a motivational command from a concerned or nervous or even insensitive doctor, who wants to get the job over and done with. But here's what I think; since it is the last action our mothers had to undertake to bring us to see the light of life…., in fact, it is the first word that keeps ringing through our ears as we step into life.(I think it is the rapturous echo following the shout of that command that make us all cry at birth. We just couldn't bear the noise.) I therefore make to believe that there is something about the word push that we shouldn't really take for granted. It is the first word we got to hear! During our birthing process we were welcomed with the word 'Push!' don't ever forget that. Therefore, in order to make things happen, you have to push and keep pushing. But hey, push with clarity and understanding. Well, this book will also help in that area. To give you an important handle for reading and understanding this book, look at that word 'Push'. Take out the first letter, which is 'P' we are going to make some amazing discoveries out of it. Hey, P is for *Passwords*. And that's exactly what we need, to survive and walk through life.

Ever noticed how successful people relate their success in life with a sentence, word or phrase? Most times we feel they are not saying all there is. But that is it. In *Passwords*, I want to give you the basics that you've been looking for, to help solve the success puzzle. I must confess the ideas here are plain practical. You are not really expected to read it until you are willing to practice it. Or to put it better, the ideas here will demand a practicing from you. So, consider if you are willing to put up with something new, simple and powerful. Okay then, here's the book for you.

I desire that this book points the way to the missing piece. That it empowers you with the knowledge that will add a little more color to your efforts. That it will be a thought provoking success workbook and as you read, you'll be enlightened by these principles to further think of other related principles necessary for your success.

KEY 1 - PERSONALITY

PERSONALITY

"... For he observes himself, goes away, and immediately forgets what kind of man he was". James 1: 24

HAVE you ever observed and wondered at how the success stories of famous people correspond with their lifestyle and personal beliefs? Nelson Mandela once rejected a college leadership position even at his own expense because he felt the process violated the majority opinion. Little did he know that his life will be about freedom fighting. According to Jim Rohn, "Success is not to be pursued; it is to be attracted by the person we become." Your personality refers to those unique attributes and character of yours that define you and cannot be confused with another person'. A person's personality can be inherent, coming from natural, biological factors and can also be formed and shaped. Your personality is your trademark. It is important you shape it or form it in order to have a strong presence necessary for success. Some people think that their attitude and traits are hereditary and therefore they can do little or nothing about it; while also upholding the view that those with a better attitude and traits must have inherited them. Of course this indifference to attitude and traits, whether good or bad is more an issue with the mind than a reality to associate with. A lot has been said about the mind's power in shaping and forming our personality. I say, "We mind our world by how we live in the world of our minds". One of the most infamous and thought provoking quotes ever, about the mind, is "as a man thinks in his heart so is he". A person is not different from his thoughts. He is defined by his belief system. If you must develop the strong personality necessary to turn success from dreams and wishes into reality, you must turn to the incredible strength of your mind to modify your reality and form new paradigms to life. Your personality is defined by two basic things;

1. Who you are (your natural and environmental realities)
2. Who you think you are. (Your thoughts)

Who You Are

It is up to you to desire success and to actually succeed. Success is a personal decision, influenced by your knowledge of yourself – self discovery. Self discovery comes through self analysis. First consider, "Who am I"? What beliefs form my drive? The foundation for building this structural edifice known as success is you - your person. By personality, I do not refer to the superficial elements for success that the contemporary society advocates for people (The personality ethic). Rather I am concentrating on the inward values that make a person. Ask yourself, "What values do I possess that can materialize my dreams?" David Starr Jordan puts it this way, "there is no real excellence in all this world which can be separated from right living?" Who you are is the foundation for what you become and achieve. When you look at the values that matter most to you, values like Honesty, Integrity, Diligence, Courage, Faith, Forgiveness etc., you can tell who you are. We are all reflections of our belief systems and values.

WHAT VALUES DO I UPHOLD?

THE STRONG ASSERTIVE self (personality) that enables success is also formed by our skills and abilities. A musician is defined by music, an athlete by sports, a writer by literature etc. In order to succeed, you must define who you are by the skills and talents you possess. If you want to succeed you must consider what you are talented enough to do that will bring about your desired success. Most people get frustrated when they think they can do something but apparently, don't receive the appraisal and compliments of the people. It is one thing to think you can do something and another thing to actually do it. If I was to offer a solution measure to someone lost in-between thinking what he or she can do and actually doing what he or she thinks, I'll say, what can you do so well that somebody else can learn something new from or see something unique in? Have you recognized your distinguishing talent or skill? The key to success is excellence. You succeed because you are outstanding in a field having many competitors. Strive for mastery!

What are my natural or acquired skills?

Take a look at these two statements, which most likely are familiar to you: "Show me your friend and I can tell who you are", "Birds of same feather flock together". What these reflect is that we pattern our lives after that of those that influence and attract us the most. What we continually see and imagine (associate with), we are likely to become. If you identify the external sources that influence your life, you can harness them to obtain maximum result. My natural skill and talent is reaching out to people: teach, preach, sing. I derive joy and fulfillment doing that. Those who influence me the most are speakers seeking to impact people's lives. There are people in other fields I admire greatly. For instance, I admire footballers a lot and sometimes I imagine myself being that too, maybe for part time. But if I am to make the most out of my natural skill and talent, I have to really concentrate and harness the resources and wisdom of those with whom I share natural skills. Now you get what I mean, right? You improve on your natural skills by associating, admiring and learning from people with related skills. Ever heard of What Will Jesus Do? A particular President of the United States was said to always ask himself when facing a difficult situation, what will Abraham Lincoln do? His answer to himself would always brace him with the attitude needed to face the situation.

What are the external influences of my life?

Our emotional makeup is fundamental in defining and forming our personality. How much of yourself do you know, emotionally? What emotional state favors you most or should I say, helps bring out the best of you? And how do you work at it or avoid contradictions to your best emotions? What are your defining reactions? What stimulates them? Successful people learn to manage their emotions and harness them to be more productive. They first discover themselves in the light of their emotional makeup and then work on their emotional trends to ensure great, quality results. A person's emotion is that aspect of his natural makeup that is responsible for his feelings, reactions and reasoning. To prepare for success you must have a good understanding of your emotional self. You must reckon with the factors that influence your emotions and how they influence it, whether positively or negatively. (Tim Lahaye's 'Spirit Controlled Temperament' deals with that.)

What is my emotion like?

LIKE WE HAVE ALREADY ESTABLISHED, who you are is of paramount importance to your success. The Bible states, "And God said unto them, be fruitful and multiply..." Genesis 1:28. Fruitfulness here implies personal productivity. God's first command to man was to be productive, starting with himself. For you to be productive, you should first deal with, "Who am I?" You are your first assignment. Who you are and who you grow to become are your primary responsibilities. The best help we can give ourselves is to know ourselves thoroughly; knowing what is available and what is lacking.

HERE ARE three all-important knowledge that every individual must arm themselves with:

Who you are. Take an introspective study of yourself. Know yourself from inside out. Your values, your interests, your emotion and what stimulates it. What's your attitude like? Getting to know yourself is an honest evaluation of your 'basic' self which is foundational to your advancement.

Who you know. Who you know is an indispensable chain in success. Every problem requires a professional for its solution. If you are to advance to the next level, you need to know people who operate in your desired level and are willing to assist you. Again, they must be willing to commit to you. It's not enough to know someone who has something to offer, you have to know someone who can offer what they have. The beauty of success is that success sterns from how much we can manage people. A good people relationship is fundamental to success.

What you know. Knowledge is said to be power. Author and Motivational teacher John C. Maxwell, always tells the story of how his parents paid him to read while growing up as a boy. I guess today it's his turn to pay back because the deal paid off. What you know is as important as character is to success. If you have character without knowledge, you attract goodwill, which on its own is good but not enough. If you have knowledge without character you cannot sustain your success. And of course, success not sustained is no success at all. So, arm yourself with the necessary professional knowledge required to succeed.

Who you think you are

Success is never impersonated. People often confuse thinking in the light of your dreams with assumptions and impersonations. They therefore develop an unduly assertive or impersonating attitude which is detrimental to their realizing their dreams. John Maxwell in his book, *The Difference Maker* says: "If attitude were everything, then the only thing that would separate me from a successful singing career would be the belief that I can do it. But trust me there is another factor that stands in my way: talent. If you've watched the reality show *American Idol*, then you know what I mean. I am amazed at the number of terrible auditioners who respond to blunt criticism from the judges by saying things like, "I know I can sing. That's just your opinion." Truthfully, no attitude is strong enough to compensate for lack of skill."'

There are two damaging attitudes — outward expressions of inward thoughts and feelings: *Exaggerated abilities* and *Undermined abilities*. People with exaggerated abilities are those who make no room for growth. They delude themselves. They shy from honest analysis of themselves and the reality they assume. Their attitude is not proportional to their reality. On the other hand, those that undermine their abilities are those that will often see their talents and abilities in the light of nothing compared to the 'greats.' They need to be consistently and constantly nudged on to believe in themselves. In reality, they have the talent and ability but they don't see it as good enough.

Defining Principles

We have established that the foundation for success begins with the person and his knowledge of himself. This brings me to a vital concept in the subject of personality —Principles. Who are you by the things you do? Principles are guiding rules adopted by knowing what is right and appropriate for you. Principles produce character which largely concerns what you do and how you do it. Your ability to regulate your life by principles improves yourself value. The sacredness to us that gives us the sense of importance that we feel and get to express, is in our enacting and enforcing guiding lines that we cannot cross no matter what.

Principles are like fences over a building that wards off unwanted animals and persons. Simply put, right principles defend our life. It could be as simple as, I must brush my teeth twice a day or I must wake up every day by 5a.m or more demanding as, I must be home before 7p.m every day, No sex until marriage etc. Whatsoever your principles are, it should be for defense and effect. Principles pattern our lives.

Like we have earlier noted, principles produce character while character creates impressions. People's opinion of you will be based on what you do and how you do it. The impression we create by our character determines who admires us and who rebuffs us. Whatsoever we do concerning ourselves, we should aspire towards positioning ourselves for what we want. Therefore, our principles should be finely blend that it would affect our social life positively and also regulate our personal lives. Some people feel that to be principled is to be mean, selfish and reticent. They relate it to minding their own business thoroughly and having a poor social life. No! Being principled does not imply having a poor attitude. In fact, your attitude is everything; as Jeff Keller puts it. Why is it so important? As you walk through this life, one thing that can ensure your happiness and joy is a right attitude. The great teacher taught us to bless those that curse us and do good to them that hate us, Luke 5:44. Why did Christ Jesus prescribe this? So we can live in this world with the right attitude. He did not hesitate to give us the balance to this affable attitude. Concerning His relationship with people, John records, "But Jesus did not commit Himself unto them because He knew all men" John 2:24. This principle was for defense against sycophants, flatterers and exploiters who seek for personal gain by appearing friendly. William Shakespeare in his words advised, "Be courteous to all but committed to few". So, form the right balance. Have a good social life but be discreet where and when necessary.

Someone may ask, "How can I get to adopt positive principles and live by them?" Every day we are faced with choices to make, decisions to take, people we meet. Principles largely concern our decisions in the face of multiple option, to have positive effects on us and preserve our sense of self value. First, be conscious of yourself; your values, dreams etc. Your decisions will fall in line with these and they will in no doubt be positive. Anthony Robbins once said, "...lots of people know what to do but few people actually do what they know. Knowing is not enough! You must take action." Are you ready for action now? Grab these help cues for developing and keeping positive principles.

Discipline

THIS IS your ability to construct yourself into what you want. Discipline deals with you. You see, success has a pattern. Whether it is success as a Preacher, a footballer, musician, etc. whatever field it is, they follow similar patterns. Your level of discipline determines the success level you will operate in. Most people are concerned about their desired success status (who they'll be following their success); the most important thing rather, should be personality concerns. It is who you are that ensures success and it is who you are that will manage who you become. When you discipline yourself to the level of an inter-continental champion, you will most certainly operate at that level. Let me expound this talk on inter-continental champions.

THERE ARE BASICALLY four success levels:

THE LOCAL CHAMPION. The local champions are those who have conquered their immediate environment. People at this level are champions within their immediate environment. From their houses to their neighborhoods and at most their cities. Their sphere of influence is majorly within their immediate environment.

THE NATIONAL CHAMPION. These are champions who have conquered their nation- state. They can be reckoned with anywhere in their country. For instance, Nigeria is a country with 36 states. People who are champions at this level cannot be strange names in any of the states within the country.

THE CONTINENTAL CHAMPION. You can possibly guess those at this level. They are the big names of any given continent. Their sphere of influence has gone beyond their countries. For instance, the President of Nigeria is nearly as popular and influential in Africa as he is in Nigeria. They are the icons of their continents.

THE INTERCONTINENTAL CHAMPION. Intercontinental champions have conquered their world and the continental boundaries involved. They are innovators. There is a distinction to their belief system that makes them great. People at this level do not follow mediocre routines. They stretch themselves beyond normal. Their goal is unequalled excellence and their limit is nothing. Their names become trademarks. They apply incredible measures in order to do incredible things. Inter-continental champions do not inherit their Inter-continental influence. It cannot be handed down by ancestry. You operate at this level only by personal drive and desire. You have to 'construct' yourself into an Inter-continental icon.

It is interesting to know that both local and national champions can be handed by ancestry. However, continental (except in few cases) and intercontinental champions do not inherit their influence over their world. They work it! And this calls for discipline.

Decisiveness

THIS IS your ability to make important positive decisions even where it affects people and other secondary issues, without sentiments. When you discover the measures, you must take in order to operate at your desired level, you must be decisive about it. While discipline deals with how you construct yourself into what you want, decisiveness deals with how you stand by your decisions no matter the influence which would mostly come from people.

One time I was addressing a congregation and I illustrated how decisiveness works; with a simple analogy. I asked, 'If you were to be a taxi driver; and as the case should be, you have designated routes for each day. Would you change the route you purposed to ply because a passenger seems desperate to go by another route?' Asides being a

Good Samaritan you'll definitely answer, no! Your reason would be based on the fact that you had made up your mind on the routes that will best suite you even before seeing anyone. So, refusing to oblige this passenger by going his or her way should not be taken personal. That's how decisiveness works. You stick with the decisions that will bring you fulfillment and success. If people feel hurt in the process, your disposition should be unaffected.

Determination

DETERMINATION IS the strength and willpower to do the first two Ds' mentioned. Be determined to go all the way. Your physical body could be the greatest odd you will have to face but by determination you will most definitely conquer it. Empower your desire! To operate at the intercontinental level, you most certainly need determination which simply is 'Empowered Desire'.

Many times, people will try to question the rationality of your decisions, like I have experienced. At such times, you could begin to doubt yourself and almost reconsider the importance of some of your decisions. Don't worry, stick to your decision. A singer once sang "It's my life, my world". Though there are two sides to this statement, but it is unquestionably true that your life is your assignment and you make of it what you want. Be conscious of the personality of life. You were born not really by your consent and approval, but your right to life and survival is exclusively yours; you don't share it with anyone. When people question our important positive decisions, often times it's because they substitute what is most important for what is less important.

KEY 2 - PURPOSE

Purpose

".... My meat is to do the will of him that sent me and to finish his work".
John 4:34

THE SEED of success is purpose. Other elements are nutritional factors that aid the seed's growth. Purpose is the seed. How you go about it is the plan and the fuel necessary to bring it to fruition is the passion.

The Lord Jesus had twelve disciples, many of who were skilled in the art of sailing the boat and catching fish. He needed such men because he must travel, and they would help him sail to the many cities he wished. He would also mount on their boats to have some of his meetings on or across the lakes. Though He is all powerful, he clearly exemplifies the view that we ought to create an environment that suits our purpose. What you watch, what you read, what you listen to: Do they line up with your purpose? What about your friends – are you attaching sentiments to your relationships even when they don't blend with your purpose? Purpose just like life, is personal. Your purpose should be the benchmark for your considerations and actions. Your actions should be weighed on the scale of purpose. Many times, people are involved in things that don't relate to their purpose; or relationships that they cannot vouch for its destination, yet they decide to stick with such, for the purpose of passing-time. I caution myself to 'leave the appetizer so I won't lose appetite for the real meal'. With the consciousness of purpose, you won't spend your time meddling with things less dignifying and apparently different from your goals. Some people erroneously think, 'I know what I am doing'. That sounds like wisdom. But the truth is that anything you accept which is not in line with your purpose and desire will eventually kill your drive. Take actions consistent with your destination.

Sometimes, people have difficulties discovering early what their purpose in life is. The creator has some ways of helping us discover this. There are early indicators and hints to purpose. For instance, people who grow to become professional writers, musicians, athletes etc, could trace their interest in their vocation back to their early childhood. Often times we reflect our life's purpose through our childhood interests and activities.

At other times also, purpose could be reflected in what we dread the most. Many people who go on to become exceptional public speakers can well recount when public speaking was their biggest and strongest phobia. They liked the idea but couldn't see themselves as fit for it. They would often feel that the stage is bigger than them and the thought of doing that seems larger than life. But interestingly, that's what purpose looks like. It is often beyond the full mental grasp of the individual who if only would keep working at it will be growing with it and fulfilling it gradually. In the Bible Gideon discovered his purpose by what dreaded the most – victimization. He hated the idea of their being enslaved by the neighboring tribe. And why was his tribe the least, his clan the least and he the last in his family? It was just to uncover purpose. The thing about discovering purpose from this standpoint is this; 'the fear cannot destroy the interest'. Once you notice an undying interest in what you fear, you may well have discovered your purpose.

Gianluigi Buffon, the famous Italian and Juventus goal keeper, didn't start out initially as a goal keeper. His story is typical of many other success stories, they stumbled into their purpose. Buffon started out as a player in the midfield position. But upon inspiration by the Cameroonian goalkeeper, Thomas N'kono, he decided to switch positions to help his team's goal-line and he was exceptional. That was the beginning of the career that brought him to lime light and announced him. Necessity they say, is the mother of invention.

Purpose is often viewed against the backdrop of what appeals to you the most, what evokes in you the greatest amount of emotion; pain or interest. It has also been largely linked to finding out what you can do best. These are very correct. Think of something that will bring you the greatest joy if you achieve it; something that you will never be bored of doing no matter how long you do it. Something that will place a demand on you to get better as you go about it; something that you will be proud of if that is all you ever did; something that you will enjoy and never give up doing even in the face of little or no appreciations or compliments from people.

The subject of purpose is the basics when dealing with success. Napoleon Hill, the famous author of *Think and Grow Rich*, who also was one of the earliest producers of the modern genre of personal-success literature, presented the idea of a "definite major purpose" as a challenge to his readers in order to make them ask themselves: "In what do I truly believe?" What the analysis and discovery of yourself will do in you is that it will equip you with the knowledge of your purpose. Your purpose will push you to meet the other demands of success like prioritizing. Purpose doesn't primarily concern itself with, 'How far can I go?' in relation to wealth and fame, but rather 'What can I do and how well can I do it?'

The beauty and importance of discovering your purpose is that your fulfillment in life is attached to your purpose. Discovering it and working at it makes you complete. Working on your purpose gives you the security that comes with fulfillment. A lot of things in life can affect our peace, satisfaction and happiness. If you discover your purpose and commit to it, it prepares you to face the onslaughts that circumstances and people can throw at you. Your purpose helps build in you a singleness of vision that makes you oblivious of distracting factors. It helps keep-out some of the negativities associated with idleness – you become too committed to discuss irrelevant issues. Realize that you cannot want to be better and embellish yourself with the elements of success without understanding your purpose.

Ronald Reagan, the 40th President of the United States of America, had a stellar career as a young man in the different fields that he delved into including acting. However, he is best remembered as being President of the United States. He found his purpose by doing 'the other thing'. He served as spokesperson for GE (General Electric) and in the course of his service as spokesperson a stronger interest was unearthed in him – politics —which went on to become the redefining turn to his life. He had found purpose.

Doing the other thing takes you through stages preempted by necessity. Here, necessity invents the platform for discovering purpose. For some people, by doing the other thing, they discover how grossly unfulfilled they are and how what they are doing hasn't proffered solution to their being unfulfilled or less fulfilled. While others by doing the other thing, find a relative stage set for them to do the main thing as in the case of President Reagan.

The Bible also accounts of Moses, who discovered purpose by doing the other thing. He was raised as the Prince of Egypt. But time revealed his apparent loss of interest and fulfillment as Prince. By doing the other thing, he had discovered what truly held his joy and happiness. It may well be his purpose! And indeed, it was. Think about the many successful people you know who steered into their fulfilling course by doing the other thing. By doing the other thing, one gives himself the benefit of doubt and gets to know his interests and to prove his purpose.

When I talk of people who stumbled into their purpose, it is interesting to note that they failed at other things. I know of a music duo in Nigeria that attempted quite a number of things before attaining stardom and fame in music. They attempted things including sports and unfortunately, failed. But it is important to note that when it comes to purpose, sometimes other things don't work because one thing has been designed to work. Sometimes people reject you because one person was meant to locate you. This is how purpose could be at times. Maybe you didn't grow with the strong hints to your purpose or are not privileged to be working on other things which could point the way to your purpose, keep working and attempting as many things as your interests can permit, you will definitely come into your purpose. What you fail at, does not really mean failure; it only helps reveal how you can be better or what you could be better at.

One very interesting thing about purpose is that purpose isn't cheap. It is highly demanding; that's why a lot of people keep working at it till they die, yet they wouldn't meet all the demands of their purpose. Life will test you to bring out the virtues necessary to work with your purpose. When you realize this, you will not give up as you strive to discover it and as you work with it. Because purpose isn't cheap, many people may not discover it early. Others after proving themselves worthy by developing the right attitude and spirit would drift into it. Others by paying the price through determination will stumble into it. While others would never discover it and may never live the fulfilled life that every soul craves.

Purpose is not cheap. If you are careless with your purpose, it will reproduce itself in someone else. I recently read about a young African woman that started a company but later lost the ownership of the company to some of the company's executives. What had happened? Maybe she wasn't a good manager. Maybe those executives thought they could handle it better. That's how far purpose can go. You have to be serious with it because it can be reproduced in someone else. Caution! People will be attracted to you because of your knowledge of your purpose and your commitment to it. If you welcome this attraction without discretion, it will lead to distraction and maybe an eventual loss of purpose. If you think that doesn't sound like something to worry about, wait till you lose the sense of your purpose; see how much value there will be to you. The world only value people who are committed to a course and are getting results.

Perhaps, not many people are aware of the true answers to basic life issues that can only be got by understanding purpose and being driven by it. Of all human issues and challenges, relationship issues mostly rank highest on the list of human problems. People often bother early in life about who their friends will be and should be, who they'll marry, what sort of people they'll like to hang around etc. In many cases, the answers most people crave don't come their ways. Why? You don't choose your friends you attract them. You don't really choose your life partner, you attract your like. "Deep calleth unto deep...." Psalms 42:7. When you concentrate on your purpose you attract people of similar interests and passion. You attract people that will compliment and value you; and that is the stalwart of any true relationship – value. If you haven't worked on your purpose so well as to reflect on you, thinking relationships will be futile. Most people, especially young people, feel a strong desire to be in close-knit relationships at the prime of their lives. They are deluded to think that an intimate relationship will help them focus and will foster greater synergy. In reality, relationships do not help you focus; you must have focus before you think of any relationship. Let me further affirm that your purpose is what you alone should decide and establish. You don't need people to help you do that. This implies that you should stay single when you are supposed to be single. The formative periods of your purpose demand your singular attention. You give it the definition you wish.

When next you think of purpose, don't think of it in the light of what can give you the biggest wealth, name and fame (I once watched a movie where someone said, "Those who called themselves Hollywood never made it in Hollywood"), rather think of it in the light of what best you can do that will bring a solution. Remember, your purpose is never about you. It is bigger than you. Think of a need you'll like to meet. Meeting it will unearth your joy. One way to solve your problem is by solving other people's problems. Also consider, "How far can I go doing this?" If it is only to enable you secure financial security, get married and live fine, rejoice! For it is not your purpose.

KEY 3 - PARENTS

P ARENTS

"Where there is no counsel, the people fall: but in the multitude of counselors there is safety". Proverbs 11:14

My early childhood was characterized by timidity, reservation and great sensitivity. Things got to me probably more than they should. It was in the light of this that I was greatly distressed when at one time some children made fun of the bag that my dad had got for me and my elder sister for school. They laughed at us because they thought the bag was quite too big for school and rather fit for travelling. So, when we'd carry them to school it was somewhat an amusing sight to them. I didn't like this. I often felt depressed and embarrassed by this. I had to keep myself from crying and at other times, cried secretly. So, I told my dad, as the children won't stop making fun of us, to get us new school bags the kind that was fitting for school kids. I told him that they were making fun of us. My father did not consent to getting us new school bags. What was I thinking? Of course, he wouldn't. We were poor! He was rather unperturbed by my pleas. But he said something that made a huge difference: "Don't mind them". That sounded too simple and if I was bolder, maybe I would have asked, "Is that all you have to say?" But it played well in my mind and it soon built in me the kind of indifference necessary to silence my mockers when I got back to school.

The words of parents stick with their children. One of the biggest source from which our personality is formed is our parents. A positive parental influence is important for success. It is one thing to have parents it is another thing to be guided by them. You never really outgrow parenting. Whoever does not have an umbrella over his or her head gets beaten by the rain. An umbrella is not luxury; it is a necessity. It is not meant for any class of people; it is for those who wish to shield themselves from the rain. Parents are like umbrellas. They shield you. They give you a sense of security. They tell you the truth that others may not.

If you do not have people above you or you do not recognize people above you, you can never move up and if you move up, you cannot be guided at the top, so a fall won't be surprising. People above us are those we value their words, consider their advice and hearken to their instructions. Remember that success cannot be attained without discipline. And you cannot be disciplined if you are not first a disciple. In life, what we really do is to grow; progressively or retrogressively. This means that we can trace our progeny. We don't just become, we grow into being. Parents are there to help us grow. In 1651, Thomas Hobbs an English philosopher writes, "Man in his state of nature is nasty, brutish and his life is short". If we are to consider this factual statement it obviously implies that man needs some taming. So, without parents, people grow by what they feel is right; which will basically stem from selfish interests and motives. And this obviously is a growth embedded on one-sided ideology or at best, an imbalanced growth. Because when placed against life's realities, it clearly shows how deficient the victim is. In contrast to growing with parents (and by extension I include: family relatives, family friends and others who hold a degree of influence over us) you'll discover that the mixture of approach, ideologies and opinions, feelings etc., combine to make you a more balanced individual. This definitely is one of the conditions necessary for human growth — physically, spiritually, psychologically, socially etc.

To every success story there is a parental figure(s). To some people these figures vary over time. Some existed for a given period of time, but these people held onto their words and instructions. An extension of this subject would consider the various roles that people above us play in our lives. Some could be coaches, others teachers, while few are fathers and mothers. Their operational nature, time and purpose, surely differ but their intended result is mostly same. Perhaps, one author who has dealt with the subject of parenting in order to fulfill purpose is Apostle Rick Menard. In his book, "As a Son with his father", he passionately talks about the parent-child relationship. This book will help anyone who desires to harness the roles that parents spiritually and physically play in relation to their success.

Sadly, to be without a parent figure in your life, leaves one vulnerable and exposed. Your parents may not always be biological. They could be your parents by adoption. Often times we hear of the father figure. But it is interesting to know that not only the male gender can play the role of a father to us. The whole concept of the father figure refers to an authority to which we are willing and humble to defer to, that commands our optimum respect and reverence. Sometimes, people we recognize as parents or would wish to play that role in us may not really be as committed to the assignment as they should. But it is not about the availability of parents and their willingness to commit to our course, it is more about our willingness to defer to superior authority. A preacher once recounted of a young man who said that when he was younger, probably in his early teenage years, he thought his father was too dumb and old-fashioned but as he grew older he was amazed to see how wise the father had become. A friend of mine once reiterated an Igbo proverb to me. She said, "What an old woman sees sitting down, a young person cannot see though standing". This is true of parents. They consider far-greater ideals and possibilities which only the humble and teachable will benefit from.

One of the biggest secrets to any success I have known and experienced is a listening ear. I can still reproduce most of the advices and instructions given to me by parents, my brothers, sisters, teachers, older friends and acquaintances, and even authors. I was able to establish at a young age that what we (young people) have is in most cases theoretical knowledge; ideas that work best in a world of fantasy, while the older people have real knowledge; knowledge that is acquaint with reality. There is a discipline and character that can only be formed in you by the influence of your parents.

It is interesting to notice that Solomon in all his wisdom surrounded himself with wise and godly men to help his administration as King, 1 Kings 4:1-6. Wisdom will teach you that there is a limit to how much you can know on your own. The prophet Joel wrote, "…. your young men shall see visions, your old men shall dream dreams" Joel 2:28. Realize by this that dreams (the foretelling of the future) is reserved for the old. When I was younger, I greatly pondered on the difference between visions and dreams. I was inspired to know that a dream is the intuition of happenings while vision is the empowerment to bring about an innovation or change. So, while the young people possess the strength and desire, the old men possess the predictable insight. In the Bible, Moses received an assignment from the Lord and was vigorous in pursuing it. Nevertheless, his father in-law who knew little about the vision foresaw by insight what could happen to Moses if he didn't put in place certain measures. He advised Moses to appoint and ordain elders who would help reduce his work load, as such, giving him room to concentrate and work on other things. Moses straight-way did as he advised, and the result was immaculate. Exodus 18:14-24

Imagine how well the story of Sampson would have ended if he constantly gave heed to the advice of his parents. It is one thing to be anointed; it is another thing to have that anointing steered to the right direction.

When I was growing as a young minister, my mother used to tell me certain things that stuck to mind. My mother doesn't give too much 'words of wisdom' but she tells you one thing in a sentence or two and will continue to repeat it until you can reproduce them in your sleep. She'll tell me, "No matter how well God uses you, never let it get to your head."

Remember that our parents see beyond what we can see. My dad has a benchmark he uses to evaluate the value of the actions we want to take. Whenever we come up with an exciting venture or idea, he'll ask you, "five years from now will this still matter?" And in most cases after sharing those ideas with him I discover that most of those ideas will lose the initial excitement that they had on me because in the light of his benchmark, they do not matter.

In Igbo traditional culture, there is a proverb that says, "One person cannot train a child". And that's true. At every stage of your life recognize and have regard for authorities that can command your attention and obedience. In college, I had people that I looked up to as my parents. I would go and discuss issues with them that I know I needed a parental advice. There is a stage you get to, it becomes up to you to want to have parents or not. What I mean is that you get to choose if you want to regard some people as your parents and who they will be. Again, in college, I didn't as much as have people who would call me and ask me how I was doing; if I was having struggles with relationships, ministry, academics, life etc. I practically sought them out where and when I needed help. As we grow older and become more mature in our reasoning, we'll discover that a person cannot know it all and may not have it all. Therefore, you need to carefully consider those who can also serve as parents to you maybe in addition to your physical parents. Realize what virtue or quality that you are yet to possess and find out who can help you. As you seek for those who can help nurture you, you don't have to go to everybody and anybody you feel, thereby turning yourself maybe, to a sorry case. Be objective! Go for the few (as the case mostly is) who will really have your interest at heart and are examples by conduct and words to what you desire. I always tell people that one of the worst positions to be in life, is the position where no one can command your fear and be a check on you against excesses.

Every relationship has a rub off. The biggest method of influence is by association. I have had to be influenced by persons with tranquil and balanced emotion, who are also prudent with their words and careful in their walk with God. When you keep a close-knit relationship with who and what you appreciate, you will in the process of time be unconsciously affected by them. My basic concept of mentorship is a close-knit relationship where the mentor teaches by conscious words and unconscious or routine actions which the mentee is left to listen and observe. A mentor should really not be far from the reach of the mentee. That's just what I think.

Surround yourself with counselors; people who you can regard as parents. They'll instill in you the virtues and counsels that make success a reality.

KEY 4 - PRIORITIES

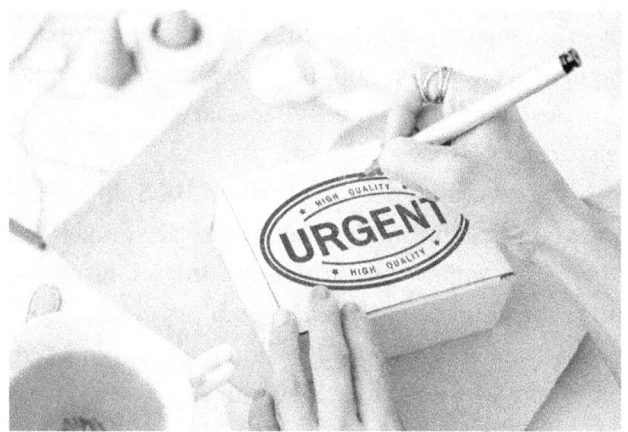

PRIORITIES

"So, teach us to number our days that we may apply our hearts unto wisdom" Psalms 90:12

'Teach us'... To live according to priorities is an art that can be learned and developed. By prioritizing our lives, we live intentionally, purposefully and accountably. To live with the consciousness of numbered days ensures that no day goes unaccounted for. Imagine how well spent your life will be if you could live circumspectly every day and take account of how you spend each day?

One of my favorite personal quotations is: "In all we do let us streamline ourselves with what is most important, that way life will be easy". Life can really be frustrating and very boring when we are unnecessarily stressed. This happens when we don't have priorities. In the computer system, there is a program known as disk defragmenter. The purpose of this program is to defragment your volumes and recover spaces lost to unnecessary folders and duplication of files. This is how priorities work. You should have a priority list. The goal of a priority list is to simplify your life by allowing you work with what is most important taking them one at a time. Also, priorities help defragment volumes in you. It helps analyze your plans, intentions and actions and sieve the unnecessary ones from occupying promising spaces.

In the previous chapter, I talked about discipline. Howbeit, I'll also like to emphasize that you cannot discipline yourself without the consciousness of what your priorities are. In fact, discipline is your tool towards achieving the prospects of your priorities.

An author once said, "Life's too short for trial and error". Most times the resources, we need to achieve our purpose are just the exact quantity. This means that if we misappropriate these resources it could take another cycle for them to come by again. If this means anything to you, it therefore implies that there is need for thoughtfulness – great thoughtfulness, in the arrangement of our priorities and our choice of what is most important.

One of the foremost principles in Economics is that of the "scale of preference." The scale of preference simply talks about priorities especially on economic issues – what to spend on and how to spend. Now, one purpose of the scale of preference is to optimize cost. To make the most out of the money at hand – i.e. minimize loses at all cost. Priorities will help you optimize cost. By attending to the most important issues first, you'll save yourself the dilemma of wasting resources on things that seem needed at first but later turn out to be unnecessary. Priority is different from goals. While priority is what matters most to you according to their urgency, goals are your targets. Priorities therefore will help you fulfill your goals. Let me further tighten your grip on the subject of priorities.

STEP 1 — Definition:
   P – Personal
   R – Rewards
   I – I
   O – Outline
   R – Regarding
   I – Important
   T – Topics
   Y – You heard!

MEANING: Personal Rewards I Outline Regarding Important Topics You heard!

WITH THIS YOU see that Priorities are to be personal and peculiar to the individual – You. Your priorities must be objective. It must have an intended goal and gain. You must be conscious of what your priorities are. Be consistent with them according to their ranking in importance. Don't misplace them or let them skip your mind. You might as well need to write them down in order to be acquainted with them. Also, you must have settled by your priority list the issues of paramount importance in your life, timing them where necessary. With your priorities carefully developed, you decide what happens and when it does, in your life.

Did you consider 'You heard!'? That's funny, right? Some people could actually think I just put it there because I had to make it complete. Well, not exactly. It's simply just right, especially considering one important aspect of Priorities, which is, your priority should be emphatic. Both to you and the people close to you, this must be emphatically stated. Emphasize it: memorize it so you won't lose it. If you're not emphatic with your priority you could actually be lured out of it.

For instance, you've carefully considered your purpose and what you want out of life. And in view of this, you came up with your priority list. On your list, relationship is to come up two years from the time of your developing your priority list. In just about six months of your deciding, settlement and acquaintance with your priority, a young man comes to talk to you about 'love'. If you're not emphatic with your priorities, it will show in your response and action. With that, the prospective lover can lure the gullible lady. Or you have carefully developed your priorities and completing your college or university education is paramount. In less than six months a business mogul comes talking to you about 'quick-money'. A less emphatic acquaintance with your priorities will sell you away cheaply. People know when a 'No' is emphatic and when it is weak; only used as an initial approach to self-worth. With your priorities carefully and effectively developed, you can always take a strong stand.

STEP 2 — How to Develop an Effective Priority List.

IT's easy to talk about priorities. But most people will find it difficult deciding what is to come first if the question 'What do you want now?' is thrown at them. Back in high school we heard so much about the importance of personal, daily time-table. We taught it was easy, but on attempt to prepare an effective one, to our greatest amazement most of us discovered it wasn't easy. Some of us ended up adopting the daily time-table of others, which off course started and ended only on paper. Building a priority list is not a two-minute assignment. For some it could take two years to really decide and discover what they want and how to go about it.

To develop an effective priority list, discover what is most important to your life. How? *By finding out what is most rewarding.* Must it be rewarding before it can be important? Yes! But it depends on what your opinion of rewarding is. Basically, the benchmark for what is rewarding is, whatsoever brings you the greatest joy and fulfillment. Why is that so? You need an emotion characterized by happiness and joy to go onto the next day and to see another year.

OTHER INDICATORS to what is most rewarding are:

- Is it of benefit to others?
- Can it grant me some security: financially, socially and mentally?

FURTHER, you have to know your passion (likes) and attach importance to things that line up with your passion. After having checked to see what is most rewarding to you, you manage your passion accordingly. What this means is this, your passion should very well work in tandem with what you find most rewarding. let's say you find helping people or missions very rewarding but you are passionate about sports they both will suffer. You cannot sustain any because your passion will require your attention, and what you give attention to will demand your passion.

Howbeit, your passion must be hinged on right values. Wrong values produce wrong results and create negative impact.

Then again, you must consider: What has the most lasting value? There are issues of short term importance and issues of long term importance. An effective, properly thought out priority list should give greater consideration to issues of long term importance. Investors are advised to invest in assets which are ostentatious (Increases in value e.g. Gold, land). That way, they are assured of increasing returns with time. For instance, it is better to go to college and get a certificate than to learn a trade. Why? Your certificate will serve as security economically, socially and mentally. Also, it is better to acquire an asset like land than to get a car. Better to plan for eternity than to be consumed by the temporal. Why? Your salvation is your eternal security. From these examples you see how I arranged what is most rewarding by looking at their time frame. So, you think of other 'betters' and develop your priority list like that.

Surely our priorities should be arranged in their order of urgency. Therefore consider; What demands your most immediate response? In developing your priority list, look out for what demands your most immediate response i.e. what is it that if you put off for tomorrow, it could be devastating? In the hospital, people in the emergency ward receive the quickest attention, while some in other wards may not have been attended to by the doctor even after being there for two days. Why? The case makes the difference. Wherever you are and whatever you do, find out what demands your most immediate response and attend to it urgently.

HOW TO MEET YOUR PRIORITIES

Make the most of time — Ephesians 5:16

IN ORDER TO achieve your goals as they appear on your priority list, you must make the most of your time. Allocate adequate time to your issues of primary importance. If it is a priority it must be treated with dignity. Activities relating to your purpose and passion should be part of your daily routine. If your claimed passion is not reflected in your environment and in your daily routine, then adopt another interest.

Every professional footballer, for instance, has a training ground or spot in their houses and football is part and parcel of their daily agenda. Same applies to basketball players, musicians, writers etc. They live out their passions.

Remember that time is the underlying factor of priorities. The reason for prioritizing is to help channel your energy towards achieving your 'most important' within your set time. This means you are working with time, you therefore do not need distractions or side attractions. How can you avoid this? Engage your heart and engage your hand! An idle person is a vulnerable person. Earlier, we considered principles as an all-important tool in fulfilling purpose and achieving success. But for principles to be effective, it must thrive on a complementary environment. What this means is that, it is not enough for you to decide what or what not to do, there should be an environmental arrangement that should support your decision. Again I say, engage your heart and hand. Let your thoughts dwell on what you want to achieve; what you want for your life. Then, engage your hand accordingly. It's not just enough to think it and be obsessed by it, get busy also. For emphasis, idle people are vulnerable people. What busyness does is that it engages you and it strengthens you. Get busy with a worthy vocation and see how focused and time effective your life will become. Getting busy is your answer to distractions. The Bible tells the story of Nehemiah, a Jewish palace staff that had a priority and a time frame for accomplishing his purposed assignment. He had desired to rebuild the walls of Jerusalem. On receiving permission from the king to go and face his project, he met some distracters who had reasons to dissuade him from his assignment. His response to their call was not that of cursing, angry remark. He simply sent an epic message to them: "I'm doing a great work; I can't come down." Nehemiah 6:3 (The Message) It was that simple. There was no room for him to consider their calls because he was busy mentally and physically. He therefore was unavoidably indisposed.

Avoid competition

Life is personal; your priorities are exclusively different from any other on the face of the planet. Therefore, your best and biggest attention should be on them. Since your priority list is different, there is no premise for competing with any other. You cannot be up against yourself. When we compete, we mount unhealthy pressures on ourselves and become impatient in dealing with what matters most to us. Meeting our priorities no longer becomes a case of self-fulfillment but of vain show. What is most important to you is different from what is most important to the other person. When and why it is important is also different. So, where's the take-off point if you wish to compete? When you avoid unhealthy competitions, you live fulfilled.

Avoid self-criticism

As a man thinks in his heart so is he. You didn't go all the way deciding what is of paramount importance to you, only to fail or give up. Therefore, appreciate and encourage yourself as you attend to your priorities. Never feel like you are not capable of following the routine or that it is too demanding. If you must fulfill your priorities, you must of necessity see yourself as most fit to achieve it. Self-criticism leads to inferiority complex. When it sets in, you begin to doubt yourself and your abilities. In fact, you see reasons why you shouldn't believe in you. You prefer to rather believe in another person and another course. You simply believe that something is lacking in you. No! Refuse this devastating feeling whenever it tries to set in and be confident, happy with yourself and what you do.

Avoid sentiments

Separation is an inevitable course. You have to do what you have to do in order to get to where you want to be. Do not attach unnecessary sentiments to your issues of paramount importance for the purpose of pleasing or impressing people. Do not adjust what your priorities are at random in order to be accepted by some or all. If you can easily be swayed from pursuing your priorities passionately, you make yourself a pushover and nobody takes pushovers seriously.

Success is not attained by emotional feelings neither is it lived out in fantasy world. It is got by a person's acquaintance with the real principles that make it happen. Get rid of fantasy ideals and pursue the real principles that turn success from a wish or desire to reality. Sentiments are emotional feelings that keep you away from facing reality.

Avoid discouragements

An author once asked, "What would you do if you knew you wouldn't fail?" If we believe we cannot fail, it is amazing what things we will achieve. You need to guard against discouragements. When you have high self-esteem, you see yourself as capable.

Howbeit, if you allow discouragements, you make up quality reasons why you are simply unfortunate.

There are different doors to the ball room of discouragement. Yes, Ballroom! When one enters here, he or she is simply satisfied with the excuse for failure. Here, they dance away their failure, blaming fate for the unfortunate turn of their lives' cause. You hear them say things like this among themselves "we could actually make it if...." Or "we could make the difference, only if we had the opportunity. I have the Government, my family or my country to blame". Blah! Blah!

Blah! Life is what you make of it. As unfortunate and discouraging your situation may seem, if you put in a little push, an extra determination and great resilience you will see how much hope you can create that will move you on.

Here are four forms of discouragement I will like to share with you.

Harsh Discouragement

This kind of discouragement comes from your environment. Your environment refers to your location-setting. It goes from universe to continent, continent to country, country to state, state to city, city to home. Also, your environment consists of the people around you, and the influence they exert on you. Everywhere you reckon yourself with often, forms your physical environment. Your physical environment offers you the first form of discouragement. The harsher your environment; the more of a champion you can become. What you have conquered feeds your confidence. If David hadn't killed the bear and the lion, he may not have been confident to face Goliath (1 Samuel 17:34-35). When you conquer the discouragement, your environment poses on you (which could be the fiercest source of discouragement), you build the willpower and confidence that makes for further conquests.

Friendly Discouragement

This sort of discouragement as it sounds, does not appear first to be discouraging but eventually discourages. This form of discouragement is offered mainly by those closest to you. It comes with elements of thoughtfulness, sensitive concern and care. Howbeit, its ultimate end keeps you out of any prospective venture.

Those who give this put-off do so with the mindset of looking out for the individual involved. They believe they have the interest of this their loved one at heart. Statements such as, "Oh, you're too young for this now; wait till you're much older" or "Oh, this project is quite complex, can't you go for something simpler?" or "There is much competition out there, your chances of winning are limited", reveal well-meaning but harmful care. You see, by these statements they showcase a great deal of consideration and thoughtfulness and you could almost buy the idea as a welcomed innovation but that feeling of doubt discourages the individual. Now the once motivated person begins to ponder and worry about the suggested fears.

The truth is, those who offer this form of discouragement do it innocently. However, the unintended consequence is that they put the person concerned out of his or her illustrious course.

Actual Discouragement

This discouragement comes from the observance of the present situation. It stares you in the face and says an obvious and daring, "Hello!" It is interesting to know that, it is only there for the moment. When you cease to recognize it and fail to welcome its desire to exchange pleasantries, it gets angry and walks away. How do I know? Discouragements like to be welcomed by their prospective victims. As a beautiful girl glows at compliments, so does your discouraging situation grow and fortify itself when you throw compliments in form of blames and excuses at them.

Total Discouragement

Yes! This is the main event, the culmination of all other forms of discouragements. It comes from you. What you eventually believe determines your fate. Once you've lost the intestinal fortitude to go on believing, trying and daring, forget it, its game over! The game goes on once you are willing to fight on. Always inspire yourself. You are responsible for your own success or failure. Dream big! The dream world is the most expensive cinema that shows the most expensive movies yet without a 'Price tag'. You don't have to be rich in order to dream or be poor in order to dream. You just need to have your mind, your imagination. Always keep your imaginative system working.

So, close your eyes and dream. You are not charged for it. The more you see, the more you can bring to reality. If you can imagine it, you can create it. Imagination is the first assurance of creation. If in the eyes of your imagination, your intended goal is successfully realized without complications, then, make it happen!

How to Guard Against Discouragements.

When it comes to handling discouragements:

DEVELOP A POSITIVE ATTITUDE. Life gives you more of what you say and think. When you develop a positive attitude, you exert a positive influence on life and how it affects you. You protect your mind from negative infiltrations and concentrate your mind-power on awesome things. Keep working on that vision and course. With a positive attitude, your actions reflect faith and hope which rarely fail.

DISCIPLINE. By discipline you determine what you accept. If you must avoid discouragements, you must discipline yourself to stay up with what you believe: the dreams, aspirations, intentions etc. Never allow your actions betray you when the discouragements start coming. Discipline yourself not to fall down and stay down due to any mistake or failure. I will like to describe mistakes as lessons uneasily learned. So, rise up and forge ahead, they are lessons any way. Any man can fall but only a strong man rises after his fall.

The discipline to rise in the face of discouragement is one of the greatest tests of success. Don't feed your mistakes.

STEP OUT. When it comes to finances and the discouragement that comes through the lack of finances to pursue personal goals, realize that money responds to projects. One rule that governs the world is the principle of profit. Even money wants to multiply. So, make your goals strong enough to magnet resources big enough. Money is a medium of exchange. It doesn't stand at a place. You exchange ideas for money. So, what ideas can you trade for money?

ASSUME RESPONSIBILITY. When it comes to discouragements due to rejection, realize that you are responsible for your joy and happiness. Don't give anyone the responsibility or privilege of determining what emotional state you should be in. When you suffer rejection probably because your goal is taking much of your attention or because it is too lofty for anyone to buy into it, realize that if they don't see what you see, they can't believe what you believe. Bottom line: Life is personal. Don't let any form of rejection water-down your drive. In fact, make the most out of any rejection. See it as an opportunity to concentrate and if you are not rejected, then reject some things or persons yourself. The road to success is by sacrifice. Most times rejections seek to try our passion, our drive. If we don't give up and give in, we prove our drive. So, the first sign people need to prove a success mission, is the drive. And they cannot really prove your drive unless they reject you. If you give up, they'll know it probably was not a strong desire or maybe you weren't sure of yourself. If you continue, they will in most cases come to support you.

HOLD YOURSELF HIGH. Don't let anyone despise you. You are first who you perceive yourself to be. People would limit you based on their limited knowledge and perception. Don't fall for that. You mean different things to different people and your abilities are varied in the eyes of people. But you are who you think you are! Sometimes your strengths are not seen, not to talk of being encouraged but that's the road of the successful. Isn't it?

Keep a routine. **Be consistent!** You have to be consistent with your priorities and in following its demand. Avoid unnecessary, irrational and rash changes. By being consistent you build focus. Consistency and focus help you actualize your objectives one at a time in the order of their importance. The joy of finishing things one at a time gives great confidence which is an invaluable asset for success.

KEY 5 - PEACE

P<small>EACE</small>

"H<small>OW BLESSED IS HE</small>, *who leads a country life, Unvex'd with anxious cares, and void of strife! Who studying peace, and shunning civil rage, enjoyed his youth, and now enjoys his age....*" John Dryden (1631- 1700) English Poet and Playwright.

THE MIND IS the seat of all productivity. It functions effectively in a temperate mental climate i.e. a condition of mental equilibrium. You may not guarantee the peace of your society or the government of the country that you are in, but what you can ensure for success to take place is the peace of your mind. When the mind is at rest, it is most productive. Most contemporary, corporate employees and employers are trained on how to partition their mental activities to effect greater productivity. They are informed to be less emotional but more rational because emotions greatly affect the balance of our minds. Your peace is dependent on how you consciously manage your mental activities in order to reach a balance.

WHAT TO BALANCE

Balance Between Pain and Pleasure.

Both pain and pleasure are two extreme stimuli that influence our mental ecology. How we handle them requires great precaution. They both are stimuli because they come to you from your physical environment and almost always demand an immediate response. When we feel the stimulus 'Pain' and respond to it as it would demand, it throws us into the valley of despair, depression, dismay and doubt. In this valley, it is impossible to succeed. Absolutely impossible!

The stimulus 'Pleasure' tries to throw us into a wild frenzy of excitement. When we feel this stimulus and respond to it as it would have us do, we'll find ourselves at the cliffs of fantasy, fun, friendships and folly. When any of these feelings gets the better of us, we tend to react more emotional than rational. How do we make the balance? Develop a stimulus absorber; an internal check against the extremities of pain and pleasure. It could be the recollection of a painful event due to an emotional imbalance, a proverb or any wise quotation (the Bible has a lot of them) etc. the more mental and conscious checks, the better. Pleasure throws you into a frenzy that could get you anxious. For me I always remind myself that anxiety kills. I try to discipline myself to act only when I am less anxious. Also, I have list of events that I can look back and remind myself that the mistakes from those events were as a result of unguarded excitements.

Notable of them all is my grade three experience. I had been among the students that represented my school in a French competition against other schools. Fortunately, I and another kid, put up the stellar performance for my school. So, I was asked by my school to receive the gift on behalf of the school because we were runners-up in the competition. I was so excited at the thought of having to climb up stage and receive the award, so I frantically darted towards the stage. I slipped and fell, got my clothes all stained; someone else was asked to go pick up the gift. I was despondent. I had missed what for me was a glorious moment due to anxiety.

In the book of Proverbs, the wise King Solomon advised, "He that hath no rule over his own spirit is like a city that is broken down and without walls." You see, the feel of pleasure could raise much excitement which when unchecked, can lead to making dreadful mistakes and crashing from that peak of frenzy. It was only when Herod the King was enrapt by the excitement from a dance that he made an irrational offer. 1 Samuel 17:34-35

Pain on the other hand is the dreaded stimuli but the more tolerated depending on the situation. For instance, most people go through a bad break in relationship and feel they have all the reasons to feel pathetic. Unsurprisingly, they attract sympathy from well meaning friends and neighbors who would generously express their sympathies by their pitiful remarks such as, "Please don't be hard on her, you know what she has been through" or "Please, he just lost a loved one, give him some space (I couldn't agree less), but does it mean we'll have to welcome and entertain pain? Most times, we could go to the extreme in mourning a loved one or a broken relationship or any loss. But please, realize that there is a beautiful life ahead of you and you need your mind to get there. It therefore has to be at peace. People will not always be there to sympathize and show concern.

Few months Timmy graduation from college, I went through series of hurting experiences. In fact, I consider that year as my most timorous year. The year that followed wasn't much better either. It was during the course of these events that I learned that people will not always care and sympathize with you. In fact, most times they only show concern and care just to satisfy their conscience and fulfill the required rudiment. At other times, they try the best they can to help you feel okay. But it is up to you to decide to give the pain and the unhealthy feelings that come with it a quit. In light of this realization, I encouraged myself to rise above my pain and use the pain as a propeller to forge ahead. Yes, most times pain serves as a propeller. However, never and I repeat, never, approach life against the backdrop of pain. It can turn you into a cynical, unexciting, ugly-looking individual. We all have challenges we are dealing with. If you let yourself at the mercy of people's sympathy and concern in order to feel happy, you may never get there. So, develop a stimulus absorber as earlier said and you are on your way to taking total control of your mind.

Balance Between Patience and Pressure.

Motivation is good; inspiration is better. To ensure the peace of your mind which is foremost for success, you have to balance between patience and pressure. When we are overly motivated, we unduly put ourselves under pressure. This is because motivation creates an external appeal. We see what we think we can do, but not what we know we can do. However, when we are inspired, we have this internal conviction based on our analysis and knowledge of ourselves. So, we are moved to do what we know we can do. Howbeit, we have to form a balance. The danger of motivation which comes with some form of pressure is that when motivated, you believe you can, so you are fired up to move. You therefore look for opportunities or maybe even create one. When you eventually clinch the opportunity, you realize that you are less prepared. While the danger of inspiration is that you know you can, but you wait for when the time is right. You look at your abilities and you are convinced of success then you lose the necessary pressure needed to put out those abilities; almost like being comfortable with your abilities alone. What do you do then? Be a student of time. Study and analyze time. When you are inspired (confident in your abilities) ask yourself, why should I wait? Your reason(s) will determine when you should move. And when you are motivated ask yourself, what do I need? Know when you are motivated and when you are inspired. Inspiration takes into account your internal qualities (the means); motivation has the physical prospects in view (ends). Here is the guide, when you are overly patient you procrastinate and could become hesitant. And when you are fired up by promissory prospects you tend to act quickly, always firing the wrong shot. Be circumspect.

Between 'Me' and 'Them'

Throughout the passages of this book I will never hesitate to affirm as often as I can that life is personal. What you want out of life is different from what the other person wants. How you go about pursuing your dreams will also vary.

The peace of your mind is determined by the balance you make between the activities and actions of people as it affects you. People are there to make us prudent, cause us pain and bring pleasure too. But we are to choose what effect they will really have on us. People will always act based on their understanding, character and feelings. Learn how to sieve their actions and make the most out of them, especially where it affects and concerns you. You see, we cannot change what happens or how people behave but we can determine our perception and response to the situation. Our paradigm to life, people and events makes a huge contribution to our peace of mind.

One of the biggest factors that help to improve personal responsibility and a consciousness that leads to a more civil behavior is people. People are there to criticize, to condemn, to confirm and to congratulate. A theory in psychology states that a person's public action is modified by his or her awareness of people. Sometimes though, we feel people are not always helpful. This happens when they blow things out of proportion, give out misinterpreted ideas of us; when they turn assumption into facts and quickly pass judgments. Therefore, we need to strike a balance in order to make the most out of people.

The world would be boring without the gossips, stories and harsh treatments from people. Perhaps, the most hurting of peoples' actions towards us are their words. So, realize that they will talk and when they talk, if you don't form the necessary balance it will hit you badly. It doesn't matter if what was said was misunderstood or wrongly perceived, they cannot suffer the hurt you will suffer if you allow those things get to you. Understand that people's rash actions are usually prompted by these killer instincts - ego, insecurity, selfishness, self-righteousness, envy and pride etc. An innocent heart seldom passes judgments. Whatsoever people say about you, analyze them by these killer instincts; if you spot the operational killer instinct behind the words, try and make a pass for them, they are only human. This thought will help detoxify the poisonous venom of those words. However, if you can't classify those words or actions by any of these killer instincts, consider the words and take the correction thereof. The balance to our human relationships can be drawn from the words of the Apostle Paul in Acts 24:16, "And herein do I exercise myself, to have always a conscience void of offense toward God and toward men."

If criticisms and harsh treatments can't stop you, praises may. Beware of praises from people. Most people who got drunk and misbehaved embarrassingly had been spurred by demeaning praises from their companions. Praises could also come from people who mean well but praises in its very nature, if not properly handled, can destroy the praised. Praises can halt you by making you feel unduly important and self satisfied or it could be an encouragement. You alone can decide what to make of the praise. People are there to offer things; you are there to make your choice.

You need peace to build up success; you need peace to enjoy success.

In financial management and planning you are advice not to shop when depressed, hungry, tired and stressed.

In sexual reproduction, couples are advised to relax before sexual intercourse, for efficiency.

In the spiritual realm, communication with the supernatural is effective in a peaceful and calm environment, within and without.

Rash decisions produce rash results. You must be at peace with yourself in order to plan for success.

How to Maintain Peace of Mind

Asides from the balance strategy that I talked about earlier, these things can help bring you into the state of peace, calm and balance.

Be in touch with the spiritual. Although this is not basically religious book, but if I am to pass an effective message across I will not hesitate to say that when you are at one with the spiritual you will have peace. Talk to God and fears are gone. This is from a personal and practical perspective.

Speak no evil. The mind regurgitates on words. What you say, the mind processes. When we speak evil of people or things, we feed our minds with fears and insecurities. When people become the constants behind your words they have invariably become the constant behind your thoughts. You cannot succeed if you overly concentrate on other people and their businesses. Free your mind. If it's not something encouraging or beneficial, it's therefore not necessary to say them.

Be at one with yourself; enjoy your own company; be content. Spend quality time with yourself. Listen to your thoughts. Introspect, read, research, expand your mental horizon. Enjoy solemn moments! Be alone at times. Not mourning or crying and obviously not on the phone. You realize yourself in your private before you advertise yourself to the public.

Learn to love. Love is what we do to help ourselves; it releases the inward qualities that make us better persons — compassion, care, selflessness etc. To ensure mental peace learn to love, not lust. Love people and express it. There is this tenderness that comes with the expression of love that makes our mind at peace. Think about people and see good things in them. Appreciate people, love your life; take in the freshness life can offer.

Be quick to forgive. Avoid at all costs misunderstandings with people. If any should however occur, be quick to forgive. Learn to let go of undesirables. Thoughts of revenge, past hurts, past mistakes all these are mental toxins. Detoxify your mind by forgiving and enjoy the mental freshness that helps make success a reality. You don't of necessity have to go back to being close friends with those that hurt you; you can simply be friendly towards them and not be friends with them.

Learn to laugh. There is a common saying that says, 'laugh-it-off'. Imagine the huge pressure and stress we take off our shoulders when we laugh. Make a commitment not to complain, whine and murmur. Learn to communicate your feelings amicably. Laughter is good medicine for our minds to be at peace. Sometimes take a look at yourself when you laugh; you cannot look any better than that.

Don't expect much from people. We get hurt when our expectations fail. Don't build high hopes with people. Man is not infallible. With this in mind, you can accommodate people in their strengths and weaknesses. That way, you won't suffer hurts.

Do the right thing. Wrong actions haunt the mind. This feeling is known as guilt and it is a great impediment to success. Keep a resolve to live right; not to hurt people, cheat them or intentionally put them down. That way, you have nothing to fear.

KEY 6 - PLAN

PLAN

"THE BOY IS the father of the man" Anonymous

I ONCE MET a school mate of mine en route to visit a family. I didn't appreciate how he looked. He was wearing a star-shaped earring (quite fanciful!) and we exchanged greetings, but I couldn't remember his name. When we got going our different ways, I remembered him back in school. I realized I wasn't shocked to see him that way because back in school, I could say he was a younger version of what I was seeing.

A teacher once said to us, "You can never really be different in old age from who you were in your younger days." In fact, your young days will birth the older you. This also is true of plans. We are not really so different from our plans (conscious or unconscious plans). He who fails to plan, they say, plans to fail.

Your plan is your structural roadmap to achieving success. A carefully developed plan will give the first conviction of success. You see it before you actually clinch it. A plan properly articulated and promising in its nature will give you one of success' most invaluable assets 'Motivation'. Motivation is the excitement necessary to push ideas into reality. With the knowledge of 'How' (Plan) and the desire to do (Motivation), success is turned from wishes to reality.

Anthony Robbins puts it this way, "Success is 20% skills and 80% strategy". It may take you a lot of time to plan but a plan successfully executed will surely pay-off. Learn to work from the background at times. Never hesitate to ask these strategic questions, how do I get there? How do I go about this? The Bible tells the story of a man, Zacchaeus, who aware of his height devised a means to beat the crowd and see Jesus. If you arm yourself with the right plan, any success is possible. Don't be in a haste to be successful, plan your way up to success. To meet with those on top, you need a plan that will take you to the top.

Your success plan has to include the proper managing of what I call the three most important market P's; People, Place and Product.

Let's look at these markets P's individually.

PEOPLE

Perhaps, the re-occurring subject of this book revolves around people. Yes! How you manage people is foremost to success.

Most success fits are the plans of a person or few individuals but the activities of more people. Dr. Rick Callahan will always say, "Relationships house our harvest". Value your relationships; nurture them, sustain them – keep it fresh. People who are careless with their relationships aren't yet ready for success. Managing people is managing success.

There are three forms of relationships that will influence your personality and character positively – the God and people above you, the people around you and the people below you. The God and people above you command your reverence; the people around you command your regard and respect; the people below you demand your responsibility. If you show gratitude and loyalty to those above you, then be kind and courteous to those around you, compliment and be friendly to those below you, imagine how well you'll harness the benefits of human relationships for success.

Unfortunately, the activities of people have also ruined prospective success ventures. Therefore, it is important to study and analyze the nature of your relationships.

Here are three classes of people close to us. A proper placing of those close to you in their right class will help you determine how you relate, and those who matter most.

CASUAL FRIENDS. These are people we seldom meet. We tend to share an exchange of warm pleasantries with them. These pleasantries could range from time consuming gist about soccer, politics etc, to simple "Good morning, how are you?" kind of talk. The point here is that the people in this category do not hold so much importance to you after the scene is finished. Most times you don't get into a phone call conversation with them. They are just casual.

There is no similarity in purpose and passion, but you can get along quite well.

TRANSITIONAL FRIENDS. The people in this class are really important people. However, they have a limited degree of importance. Their importance is based on purpose and time. When we understand that there are transitional friends we won't try hard to be close to everybody and we won't struggle to hold onto them either.

The word transitional simply refers to a passing onto another phase. So, they are important while you all are in an identical phase, for the same purpose at the same time. Success is a chain and people are definitely part of the success process. This implies that, to some people, they'll only play a given role at a particular time and soon would lose close knit with you. An example is college undergraduates. While they are in that phase they are closely knit together. They could be course mates, level mates, reading mates and in some cases bed mates. Howbeit, when this stage is past, everyone seems to move on with only the memories. Many young people dwell in this stage. They subject themselves to unnecessary stress and pressure because they fail to realize that a relationship could be transitional. Therefore, they tend to believe that some people are supposed to be with them for life. This happens especially with intimate relationships. Love never dies. It may get cold, but it can still be warmed. It can expire, but it can still be recycled. If you are having issues deciding if a person you are intimate with or want to get intimate with is meant for the long run, give time. Lust happens to those who just feel; Love happens to those who wait.

I once had friends who were so attached to me and me to them, that you can sense me in their personality and vice-versa. However, I notice when I leave the immediate environment, the vibe usually goes. Most times I think it is my fault. Maybe I'm no longer who I used to be or no longer sound as I used to. So, I consciously try to do the things I used to do, exactly how I used to do them. Guess what? It doesn't restore that former vibe of friendship. The communication still would be formal and lackluster. At some point I conclude that it isn't my fault. This formed my resolve that a strong relationship is not a function of location; it is a function of the heart. Don't be afraid to lose friends. There may be no similarity of purpose like I've already stated, or they may not really understand your purpose and relate with you in the light of that understanding. And if they don't really understand you and what you really stand for, they won't really value you. There can be no strong relationship without value. At the transitional level, most relationships get tried. The people involved could be dealing with the five stages listed below that almost follow a strong relationship.

FAMILY FRIENDS. When the heart is knit together, the friendship never really dies. The word family does not only imply the union of father, mother, children and relatives. Family in real terms refers to those closest to you. Most people that go on to become our family friends were met at the transitional stage. Fortunately, they go into the other stage with us. At the transitional phase of the relationship, you can ascertain who goes into the family phase or who stays back. This is important for you to know so you would not run into the risk and subsequent pain of trusting and confiding in people with limited relevance to you.

THERE ARE five stages that culminate to the knitting of the soul together in an unselfish relationship.

ADMIRATION. This is the start to every relationship. You observe a quality which you admire. It could be the personality of the person, his or her looks, carriage, character or even the degree of knowledge he or she possesses; something good enough to bring you to a point where you could feel comfortable exchanging pleasantries with this person. If he or she lurks around your immediate environment, your constant admiration will somehow bring you into the pleasantry stage where you are comfortable exchanging pleasantries with them and even engaging yourself into some pet talks with them. From this point, he or she will gain acceptance with you and now you may want to be conscious of him or her to really know him, so you....

Test. The testing stage is the aftermath of admiration. After we have admired certain qualities in the people we meet, which endear them to us, we very often want to test them to see how they should matter to us. We test them against the backdrop of the values we stand for. The interests we live with and the purpose and convictions we could die for. If by our analysis, who we prove them to be does not match their public personae; we'll begin to doubt them.

Doubting. How long will this person be relevant to me? With the results from our tests, we'll begin to introspect and ask questions about the relevance of this person to us; with his or her deficiencies and strengths being carefully evaluated. Will they really matter at the long run? In light of these considerations, we'll tend to soft-pedal our relationship, so we can get the best professional answers that come with time. What we do is to give time to really prove them.

One thing about really admiring a person from the outside, especially for a quality that you perceive is this; when the quality you observe and admire, does not really match with what you later discover you feel disappointed. However, you could still want to give them another chance to redeem their image before you. That's why it is said that, 'First impression matters'. For some people they say, 'First impression is the only impression'. You only get one chance to make a first impression.

Proving. Friends will sometimes leave you to prove you and when they prove you they wouldn't want to lose you. At this stage you now have in your hands the knowledge of your friend's strengths and weaknesses. You analyze them and separate them just like a laboratory scientist. Then you consider them. If their strengths outweigh their weaknesses, they are still potentially important to you. But if their weaknesses outweigh their strengths, then that's it; end of relationship. However, if you are still undecided you will need to continue working with time. This is the stage where transitional friends are separated from family friends. If you can't prove your friend, you can't accept him or her either.

Acceptance. At this point you have done the careful analysis and you have finally accepted the friend for who they really are. Guess what? You are now family. You don't consciously decide the friend or friends who become family; fate does. You cannot also decide when you'll meet them. You just go on with life and people. When you meet them, you will know because they will be good for you and you for them.

A family friend understands you, accepts you, believes in you, respects you and loves you. There is a soul's connection with them. A family friends shares similar ideas with you, believes in related ideals as yourself & shares similar life passions with you. It is interesting to know that people in this category are not much. It takes time to meet and connect with them.

People can be good to you but not good for you. This is the difference between transitional friends and family friends.

Now that we have understood the nature of our relationship with people and how we are to sort them accordingly, let's objectively consider the qualifications for people that will be on our success team.

Who do I work with?

Team work is the beauty of success. You need people, but you don't need everybody. Identify those with similar interests, affinity with you and respect for you. Determine those you will work with personally and those you will work with collectively. These are people who you should feel safe associating with. People feed ideas; people kill ideas!

There are basically three kinds of people you should pass up;

PEOPLE WITHOUT CHARACTER. People without character are not worthy of your trust. A person without character is not a good influence on your success dreams. People like this do not feel the unbiased and impartial verdict of their conscience when they do wrong. For people like this, right things are only those things that suit them. If you cannot vouch to some extent for what they can or cannot do, then you don't need to commit so much. Character is the fine blend of qualities that make up a person's personality. A person with a good character exhibits fine and admirable traits. They are humble; so, it's easy to work with them. They are honest; so, it's easy to believe them. They are simple; so, it's easy to teach them and also learn from them. They are attentive; so, it's easy to communicate with them. They are appreciative; so, it's easy to work for them.

PEOPLE WHO ARE NOT HONEST. For me, honesty is the noblest virtue. It is the mother of a beautiful character. Dishonest people cannot be trusted. They are highly deceptive. Keep away from anything that could present you less honest than you would want. My resolve has often been to be as honest as I can possibly be. However, what amazes me at times, is how cynical people can be of people who appear or try to appear honest. Funnily, people have tended to judge me or analyze me by the color of my lips more than the content and weight of my words. So, while they tend to believe my words they feel impinged owing to the color of my lips. I've seen people who after periods of watching and waiting, boldly step up to ask me if I do smoke. I usually reply, 'no, I don't'. On one occasion someone persisted in asking me that and suggested that maybe I had quit smoking after I gave my life to Christ. And again, I'll answer, 'no, I've never smoked'. Some people when they finally get up and personal with me, knowing me well, usually confessed what they thought. Yes, I really have dark lips. In fact, sometimes I tend to think I'll believe any myth that tells me that the nurses smeared charcoal on my lips at birth. However, I've learned by this that people are watching and checking what you say and do. For some people they are watching and checking based on their assumptions of you. You have to realize this and maintain an honest stand always because *honesty does not change gear*. It keeps track and soon people will begin to follow its lead.

An honest person owns his flaws where he or she is wrong and just speaks the truth not to really impress anyone. You understand them easily and it makes it easy for you to work with them. Dishonest people complicate issues. If you want to work with honest people, be an honest person yourself. It is not the 'imperfect' man that is detested by God and man, it is the dishonest person. Honesty pays. One of the beautiful things about honesty is that it builds a name for the individual who treasures it and holds it dearly. People will give positive testimonies of you to others.

PEOPLE WHO DO NOT *Care About You*. If someone does not care about you, don't waste your time hanging around them for long. If they don't really care about you, they may never take you seriously. Now, the negative effect of hanging around someone who does don't really regard you is that you may soon begin to see yourself in the light of how they see you. Or you may soon begin to lose the full impact of who you really are. Whatsoever you say is treated with disdain and with little or no regard. People who do not care about you are not much bothered about your success or failure. You only exist; you don't live in their hearts.

I have learned that it is no use hanging around someone who does not really care about you as much, or close to how much you care about yourself. If they don't care about you, they won't believe your vision. They can't encourage your drive. They are almost irrelevant to you and where you are going.

Who do I need?

Mike Murdock will always say, "You are one man away from the next season of your life". Find out whose appreciation of you and what you do, will take you further. Get the attention and interest of those that matter, then they will make you matter. Musicians crave the attention of renowned producers in order to excel. Young professionals seek out mentors who would lend them a hand to the top. It could be a major dealer in a business, a media host, a politician, a journalist, name them. Just make sure you showcase your abilities and talents before a professional in your desired field. Their appreciation of you would be a great leap to success.

Who needs me?

Identify your people. When you identify the group of people, the class of people age or sex that will need you, you work harder to know what their interests are. You limit your activities to them. This makes for greater efficiency. Your consumers are your biggest marketers you need to identify them early.

PLACE. Location is an invaluable asset in business. Ask yourself, where am I most needed? Find a place that will inhabit your plans. In deciding your location, you should consider certain key factors;

Think of the kind of competition you will face; healthy or unhealthy competition? Will it be beneficial to you? What publicity can you get from the place? Would you be able to sustain your product in such a location? Is it safe for what you do? What prospects are in the location in general?

PRODUCT. What do I have to offer? For me this factor is of exclusive value. While people get excited and all fired up for success, only few people take time to actually ask themselves, what do I have to offer? Most people get excited about the prospects of being on stage but are rarely bothered about their performance up stage. As we therefore consider what we have to offer, these considerations are of invaluable importance.

PREPARATION. For your product to be extremely useful and highly appreciated, there must be great preparations put into it. Take professional athletes for instance; there is an obvious announcement of what they do when you come around them. Their homes, friends, time all spell, S-P-O-R-T-S. Almost all of them have their personal sports facilities like a basketball net, a small football net, a golf space etc. in their homes for constant practice. You must give daily attention to your product. It could be talking; then you'll need to read, rehearse and review talks made by others. What about music? Same approach too. What you have to offer should be your mind's chief priority. Once I watched a movie where someone asks his friend, 'How can you be in the show-business when you have no business to show?' People will accept and acknowledge you based on what you have to offer. You thrive in any place of your choice based on the value of your product. Always ponder on this question, what do I have to offer? It will help build your capacity. Don't let a day pass by without giving attention to what you have to offer. Practice your vocation until it forms your persona.

If you are not aptly prepared, you'll pass out on opportunities. My father one time said, "There will always be a first chance, but a second chance is not always guaranteed". If this should be thoughtfully considered, it implies that you should be thoroughly prepared because opportunities can show up in the strangest of places at the strangest of times.

BE PASSIONATE. Don't let a day pass without giving attention to what you have to offer. How can you sufficiently brace yourself for this? Passion! The key to making a wholesome output is passion. If you must sophisticate yourself enough to never be out of vogue, then you must be passionate about what you do. The subject of passion is an extensive subject. However, I'll try simplifying it here.

Life becomes meaningless when the passion is gone. Passion is the fire that keeps a vision running. Passion is fire! You can love but if there is no passion the love will grow cold. Passion is burning love. It keeps your interest fresh. From your love for God to your love for your wife, children, profession etc., passion keeps it as fresh as when you first embraced it. If the passion isn't there, you cannot go for long. Passion is the biggest drive for success. Passion is what embellishes purpose. The part of purpose that ensures it comes into reality is passion. Passion is possessive, and it is reflective. Passion is a constant source of inspiration. Think about the number of things you would achieve if you approached them passionately.

Pay the price

Success without a price is impossible. What price can you pay for the success of your product (what you have to offer)? Everything somehow has a price tag on it. A comedian once said that heaven is free for all, but you have to buy a Bible. Success does not have a single, onetime price to it. You pay in varying degrees and not once. In preparing your product, you have to meet the demands that would make it of inestimable value.

WHAT TO PAY for

PAY FOR KNOWLEDGE. Invest in mind exposing ventures. Pay for your mental development. Tour through books, inspiring seminars and conferences etc. Remember in our first chapter we established that what you know is proportional to what you work with and what you eventually become.

PAY FOR A 'LEASH'. A leash is a restraining device. You have to meet the demands of your product; and to effectively do that you must place a restraint on yourself and some of your activities.

For you to be truly successful you'll have to step on toes when it is called for by taking steps necessary to actualizing your vision. This includes your own toes and the toes of others.

Pay the Spiritual price. Throughout the pages of this book I present to us the spiritual side of success. Champions harness the spiritual advantage to get the edge over their contemporaries. Successful people pay a spiritual price. Pray! Pray!! And don't stop praying. If you are oblivious to the spiritual price of success or have willfully decided to be indifferent to it, then I can say you are still far from your dreams. Find out the spiritual price to pay and its consequences if there are. A lot of people know about the spiritual side to success and have deferred to their knowledge by paying some prices but didn't ponder on the consequences of their actions. In the secret 'P' I talk more about the spiritual price to pay and the blessings that follow.

KEY 7 - PROCESS

Process

"WHEN I WAS A CHILD, *I spoke as a child, I understood as a child, I thought as a child; but when I became a man, I put away childish things.*" 1 Cor. 13:11

Simply begin! Beginning is your assured platform for success. You can never succeed until you begin. What guarantees success is that a step is made in the line of your desired success. The thing about the beginning is that it is often filled with uncertainties. So many questions, so many fears. However, there can never really be a perfect beginning; so, begin anyway.

When I think of the beginning of any successful venture, one that comes to mind is how my parents began. I once looked at their wedding photo and thought to myself, 'the beginning is not always exciting.' I look at their recent pictures and now I think, 'the beginning paves the way for an exciting end.'

Successful people realize the uncertain, imperfect nature to almost every beginning, but they begin anyway. Because in the end, it is that process that makes for an exciting, successful and fulfilling end. You have to fall and crawl as a child before you learn to walk and run as a man. Nature made it that everything should follow a process. Don't be afraid of beginning. Many people get scared of beginning a thing for fear of making mistakes. There is room for making mistakes. Mistakes are inevitable stops on the way to an impactful and successful life. The wisdom of a man is gleaned, in many cases, from his experience with mistakes as a child.

Growing up, I wasn't welcoming of mistakes. In fact, I dreaded it. I just wanted to be perfect and have everything fall in place perfectly also. My great desire for perfection, coupled with my somewhat cynicisms and great thoughtfulness – I suppose, made me believe that I was very close to perfection. So, my analysis and assertions – I would think, were not totally wrong. I was wrong! I would later learn that 'perfection' comes through mistakes. I learnt that the fear of mistakes doesn't always keep you out of making them. Sometimes, making mistakes is a necessity.

If you have been patient reading through the pages of this book, you have followed a significant success pattern — Process. Success is a process. Johnny Bench, a former major league catcher once captured his story. He said, "In the second grade, they asked us what we wanted to be. I said I wanted to be a ball player, and they laughed.

In eighth grade, they asked the same question, and I said a ball player, and they laughed a little more. By the eleventh grade, no one was laughing" Why did they stop laughing? He had continued working on his ambition and undoubtedly proved he was not making lofty wishes. William Shakespeare said, "To climb steep hills requires a slow pace at first". So, if you are not patient with the process you may never get to have the results.

I learned through a rather disheartening experience that noble things follow a process. Once I tried to date a girl in college. I wasn't really schooled on how to go about the whole thing. Things were looking quite promising between me and this young lady, so I felt I should be direct and concrete about what I expected of the relationship. Anyways, I was too fast. I didn't really know of the concept of being too fast in wanting to date a person. So as expected, I failed. But I learnt something. I learned to progress gradually with the process of anything or course you desire; to be patient with the process so you can clinch the promise.

By committing to a process, I've learned that there are lessons that may only be learnt by mistakes. Even Jesus Christ never chose 'perfect' people, he chose and walked with people who were teachable; people who can go through the process. And that also is how he walks with us. The brokenness that comes through repentance is necessary in walking with God. Imagine how much of grace we will preach and relate to, if we never experienced it in our weaknesses? Imagine how prideful we'll get if we never make mistakes that will later bing us to our knees in The Lord's presence?

The process that matures us and empowers us for success takes various forms. If you've never experienced disappointments then you are yet to be on the process that will help try, prove and empower your purpose. Disappointments help test your purpose. Disappointments develop in you the right mindset that matures you. If you never got disappointed in life, imagine how arrogant you'll feel and the false belief that you'll have thinking you'll always get what we want. This is what process does to us; it matures us. It empowers us, and it establishes us. People, who give up on you as you go through your process, may not have been designed for you. The experiences you get as you go through your process, is to balance you. The cynicism and criticism from people is to prove you.

As you walk through the process to success, realize that the process may not really be what you expected. However, by clinging to your purpose you'll scale through. Many a times when I listen to successful people in business, entertainment, ministry etc. talk about how they were not accepted and wouldn't even be given a chance to prove themselves or showcase their talents, I sometimes think, 'How'? But you look smart and appealing. How could anyone ever reject you?' Well, maybe I think that because the image I am seeing is the image of who they've grown to become. I didn't get to see them going through their process. Probably, if I had seen them then, I too would have rejected them. You may also have wondered at times, why successful people were shamefully rejected. In fact, their stories of early struggles often times sound exaggerated. The purpose of this is, first, to prove that noble things follow a pattern — most times, harsh. Second, to encourage you to believe that you too can be truly successful. Don't give-up on the process; follow it till you reach the promise.

Recently, I had someone talk about the process of breaking into clean, clear, crystal waters in Nigeria. The topography in Nigeria differ amongst the different regions of the country. In the eastern region, the initial dig unearths debris from the earth including, human and animal fossils. The next phase gives water. But this water however, is largely unclean. It turns from its initial crystal look to a blue-black color following the 1-day test. Then, the final stage breaks the crystal stone. The crystal stone is the stone that seals the crystal waters. Once broken, access to clean, clear water is guaranteed. This process is typical of the process to success. The first real attempt you make at success, you could be faced with harsh realities including indifference and cynicism from people which can make you back out — similar to the unearthing of unappealing human and animal fossils. A further thrust will see you make some reasonable leap. But it is nothing compared to what you really want. At this point, you tend to meet people and situations that are quite considerate. They consider you and may feel to help you. Some could want to but may not really have the means to do so, so they offer their little help. Others could help out of pity or a plain attempt to satisfy their conscience, while others make promises they can only hope to fulfill. You need to thrust more. At the final stage of your thrust, the crystal stone stage, of course you have mustered enough courage and strength from deep within you to push past any oppositions, limitations or fears. Though it will require more effort, you are willing to give it your all. Once broken, eureka! You have found it. The phenomenal thing about the crystal water is that it cannot be corrupted by debris. Once you've gone through the process to success, your past pains cannot keep you out of the joy of your achievements. When you break-through, life becomes more easy. It is interesting to observe how that before becoming a success, your birthday may be forgotten by friends and family, and then on clinching the goal, you make headlines. Your birthday is carried in the media and almost on every social network, without your prompting. It is also celebrated even in your absence. For example, I recently heard them announce and make jingles over the radio stations in Nigeria over the birthdays of some foreign personalities like footballers and musicians, even without their knowing. They did it for free! That's what it feels like to prove your vision – people celebrate you beyond your grasp. At this level a sentence you make becomes a considerable issue, topic or quotation in contrast to when people will not even complement you by taking notes over your long hours of talk.

The knowledge of yourself and your capacity for greatness will push you past the limitations to success. The Bible accounts of King David's three mighty men who opted to fulfill their king's wish to have his thirst quenched with the waters from the gates of Jerusalem. Though they were to cross over the garrison of their enemies to fetch him the water, they asked him to relax while they went and got it. What gave them that overwhelming confidence? They had assessed themselves and have proved their drives, that they cannot be quelled by any limitations. Friends, by determination and perseverance you too can break-through!

As you go through your process to success, don't give people room to disregard you or take you for granted. Don't turn yourself into an object of pity; appealing for help in the most dehumanizing way. Treat yourself with dignity and give people reasons to treat you that way too. Your integrity and dignity are vital to your success. Don't go into any unaccepted alliance that will risk your integrity and jeopardize your success.

Every noble thing follows a pattern. Here is a pattern that most noble things in life follow.

Play

Every vision, dream, purpose or profession may all have begun as a play. First, people will think you are joking. Or maybe you wouldn't really take it seriously yourself, thinking it only a hobby. Most noble things in life begin against this backdrop.

The classmates of Johnny Bench felt he was joking when he said he wanted to be a ball player. Probably, he didn't quite look it or was not really good at the sport, but he believed in his dream. Success favors the simple; people who are not afraid of making mistakes, people who are not satisfied with average and not ashamed to learn more. They start out pathetically, with people laughing and gagging at them but they continue with this 'joke'.

I look back and I remember some tragic memories of some of the things I reasonably do well now. For instance, in my first year of senior high school, I was flogged because I couldn't boldly face the crowd and speak up during a course seminar. Also, in grade four, although I was in the debate team, I could only maintain my focus before an audience by facing downwards. I could think of lots of other instances. But today, (although every public speaker still deals with stage fright depending on the stage), I have well conquered those limitations.

Like I've already stressed, keeping with your vision might to some people be a joke. You could even think that way at times. But just continue playing and see how far the play goes. Once your interest is there, don't kill it and don't give anyone room to do it either.

Pressure

What probably was a hobby may well begin to develop some form of attachment to you. At this point you feel obliged to pay attention to this hobby of yours. It has now become an inseparable burden in you. Many of the success stories we know, bolted out of school because they could no longer manage the burden of their purpose. They had to give it more attention. It literally took over their minds; it needed a birthing-forth.

Maybe you liked singing for fun, now you really desire to be in a choir or sing in a concert or even come up with your own album. What you formerly couldn't understand or maybe didn't really take seriously is now having a strong bond with you. The pressure grows so much and soon you'll begin to feel you'll be better off with the outcome of this pressure. Now you want to own this pressure; you want it to become a part of you. Then you....

Push

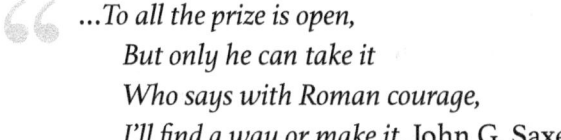
> ...*To all the prize is open,*
> *But only he can take it*
> *Who says with Roman courage,*
> *I'll find a way or make it.* John G. Saxe

Push! Push!! Push!!! A familiar command isn't it? It is a universal command to pregnancy ordering it not to hold back its new from coming into reality. Now, you are comfortable with what may well have started as a play that you want to give birth to it and make it your life's vocation. It will no longer come on you as a strong desire or interest; it now becomes what defines you. It becomes your life; what you are willing to live for, live by and what you are willing to die for.

The thing about pregnancy is this; once its pressure is so strong, delivery can take place anywhere.

This should be the attitude of anyone who wants to birth this one-time hobby that has grown to become an inseparable desire, to say with utmost Roman resolve, "I'll find a way or make it". Terence Publius once said, "Fortune favors the brave." When you push you must persist. It never takes a single push to birth a child. Once you identify with what you are willing to spend the rest of your life doing, then you are well headed for this destination...

Praises

Whatever you commit to, should yield positive results. Commitment is the key of results. Purpose and passion produce results known as praises. Purpose + Passion = Praise. Once you are passionate about your purpose you must definitely make huge success; and the outcome is praises from people. There is no luck in success. It is just purpose, plan and determination.

For anything to be, it must first go through a process. To position yourself for the process to success, first be;

1. *Simple*: Be open to learning. Be open to acquiring new ideas. The value of your life depends on your capacity to improve. Nobody knows by thinking they know; people know by realizing how much they don't know.
2. *Be committed to using what you know*: Put your knowledge to work. Success is not proved by just what you know; it is seen in the results you obtain from what you know.
3. *Understand the process of growth*: You don't become a professional spontaneously you grow into one. So, don't be ashamed of making mistakes; a child must first fall and rise for his or her legs to grow strong. This is how nature has made it, you grow into maturity. This also implies that as you grow older – literally and figuratively - you outgrow

some things less befitting of you. Don't repeat certain childhood mistakes as you grow into adulthood.

4. *Don't rest on your laurels*: There is no limit to excellence. So, don't stop where you are applauded, go ahead. In his book, talent is never enough, John G. Maxwell pointed out to a 'P' which I would like to refer to as I conclude this chapter, and it is PLUS. Add to everything you know and do. That is what success really is; strides in the now, not feats of the past.

KEY 8 - PRACTICE

P RACTICE

"W̲ʜᴇʀᴇꜰᴏʀᴇ.... *brethren, give diligence to make your calling and election sure; for if ye do these things, ye shall never fall:*" 2Peter 1: 10

SUCCESS IS ESTABLISHED on practical principles. The game of Champions is practice. Practice is a proof of diligence. Diligence can only be seen in how much you improve on what you do. No one is born perfect in his or her field of interest. So, you have to practice until perfection. Practice they say makes perfect. The famous United States Baseball player, Reggie Jackson, once remarked, "A baseball swing is a very finely tuned instrument. It is repetition and more repetition then a little more after that".

Consistent practice is the open secret of world class performers. By practicing success principles, we turn them from theories to realities. Don't just know, try doing and make action a custom. When you keep up with what you do by practice, you eliminate the fear of failure. Adequate practice can make you only one thing; Better! The nature of the world is growth. There is no highest height. If you don't make yourself better you will not matter. If you don't make yourself better, you will be inferior to those who have made themselves better. If we don't improve by practice, we become redundant. And guess what? Life and people will gradually pass us by.

Sometimes I hear people complain that an old friend or acquaintance has become successful and appear not to think of them. On hearing this many people who are more emotional than rational will accuse the fellow being talked of, of being selfish, egocentric and less caring. However, a better analysis will show you that, as a person grows, he grows into bigger responsibilities which certainly imply that he outgrows some things. If you don't improve on yourself and what you do - by practice, you'll go down on the value and acceptance list of those that matter. Never you be deceived, people's care and appreciation of you is directly proportional to your relevance. The Bible quite frankly tells us that the man diligent in his business shall stand before Kings he shall not stand before mean men. You see, consistent practice brings promotion.

Ever wondered how some movies and songs no longer captivate us that much as we grow older? In fact, we could gladly pass up on them now, which was unthinkable sometime ago. That's because they can't get better than what they had already been, so we've outgrown them. Consistent practice keeps you relevant. Your relevance is lost when you don't improve by practice. The world doesn't seem to care much about mundane people and ideas. If you feel people value you, wait till you don't seem to get better at what you do, and then see how much value you'll get.

There seem to be a slight similarity between the keys *Process* and *Practice*. But, the process to success deals with bringing you into success while practice deals with keeping you up with the success. True success is success that grows. If you don't practice you will soon be out of practice.

Initially, regular practice could be boring and tiring, but if maintained it will become an interesting routine. Every practice brings an added boost to confidence. I once heard the story of a blind keyboardist who for some reason was sent to prison. In prison, he consistently visualized the piano and playing it too. After some years, he was released to be united with his piano. To the utmost surprise of many, it appeared he hasn't even been away from playing the piano; he didn't lose the touch and wasn't making mistakes due to a time – off. Later, he was asked how he was still so exceptional with the piano. He explains how he never ceased to play the piano even with his mind.

Mind! Can we talk of the mind's role in success? One factor for success which has been greatly campaigned for from the 19th and 20th centuries is the vast power of the mind and imagination in achieving success. 'Where a man's heart is, there his treasure lies', 'as a man thinks in his heart so is he' are some of the scriptures that reveal the mind's power in making success a reality. Practice should first be imagined. Your imagination of it is what makes for improved innovations and invention. Always imagine the big stage for your vocation; the dread of disappointment will push you to always practice. Imagine you are a singer and you are to sing in a mega event holding in one of the big stadiums with flash lights glittering over and focused on you, then suddenly your voice cracks or you don't get your pitch right. How dreadful! You see, when you imagine the big stage you look out for pitfalls. This will propel you to practice and practice and practice until you are sure of success. The question champions ask themselves as they practice is, "How can I do this better?" I've already said that you shouldn't let a day pass without thinking of what you have to offer. Get better or you get beaten!

Interestingly, the subject of practice cannot be overstretched. The message is simple; always keep in touch with the talent that house your value. It largely concerns doing more than it concerns saying. So, take the nudge from me, go get better at what you do and see how far you'll break limits.

KEY 9 - THE SECRET 'P'

THE SECRET 'P'

"*He who dwells in the secret place of the Most High shall abide under the shadow of the Almighty*". Ps. 91: 1

"Yet as a rule, there seems to be a connection between professional performers and the spiritual side of life" – Steve Siebold, *'77 Mental Toughness Secrets of the World Class'*.

The spiritual realm is a beautiful realm that cannot be fully described by words. Individual experiences in this realm cannot be vividly described. An attempt to convey the experiences in this realm may not be clearly comprehended by the logical human mind. So, it is better experienced than expressed.

To every physical success there is a spiritual influence. Every man has a spiritual touch upon his life; this spiritual factor is also known as aura. It is the sub-conscious, unseen presence that looms over us, which affects how we are treated. In reality, people treat us based on the sort of presence and aura that we exude. They themselves are not conscious of it; they are also influenced by the presence over them in dealing with us. We prefer someone over someone else or even get preference ourselves based on the aura we exude. Why, because every relationship must have a rub-off. Every relationship must reflect on the parties involved; spiritual relationships no less. This is why people should consciously decide what presence they want to loom over them or any presence will. Some spiritual presence only causes havoc and wreck. They annihilate the privacy and peace of the individual they've come upon and place on them such aura that makes it almost impossible for this individual to succeed. People's perception of you is based on the aura you exude. This is why most times some people are misrepresented or given a negative impression. People who are unaware of the spiritual side to life and success, become victims of circumstances. Don't be deceived; life is more spiritual than physical. Therefore, be careful to know what spiritual influence looms over you. You can either contract a spiritual influence or presence by association, or you can attract one.

The Presence of God is the single most powerful definition a man or woman can attach to his life. It is the master key of success. It is so powerful, the knowledge and experience of it can single-handedly transform you into a success beyond your widest imaginations.

The Presence of God is the hovering of His Spirit. The Spirit of

God is the finest treasure that mortals can possess, (2 Corinthians 4:7). To the unlearned, He teaches. To the timid, He empowers. To the unsuccessful, he makes prosperous. To the rejected, he makes a king. He is the best transformational factor to mankind. The presence of the almighty satisfies you. The introductory quotation to this chapter, tells us that those who dwell in the secret place of the Most High, shall abide.... Notice the Words, 'Dwells' and 'Abide'. It is interesting to know that many can enter a room or building where Christ is preached and God is glorified but only a few really dwell in His Presence. That is why this Key is a secret or I should say an open secret. This presence is not a place we enter and leave unceremoniously. It is a place we dwell in. once you have experienced it, you can never want to do without it. It becomes the hunger of your soul. It satisfies you. It becomes the secret to your illustrious success.

In Psalms 71:7, King David says, "I have become as a wonder to many, but you are my strong refuge." David in essence was saying, I am celebrated but the secret is you. The presence of God enables you to walk in the grace of God. A supernatural influence takes over your natural abilities. Imagine how successful you'll be, if there is a touch of the supernatural upon your natural? As the shadow is attached to every individual, so also is the presence of God a shadow for those who dwell in His Presence. He does not let them be alone. Ever wondered how many people will put in the same effort and do the same thing but get different results? Some people get more impressive results than others. The secret is grace. Early inter-continental champions realized this and took advantage of it. They didn't want to do without it because really, they couldn't do without it. Moses, the Bible accounts, couldn't go without the presence of God. Gideon also, was a timid man who when he came in contact with the Spirit of God, became extra-ordinarily bold and strong. Samson, the famous personification of strength, had this presence with him and continued to make a difference in his generation and tribe, as long as the presence was with him. Jesus Christ said, "...for without me you can do nothing". This also implies that with me you can do anything and everything. To some people these words of Christ seem to only be a claim. But others who believe and embrace this 'claim' have come to prove it as true using their lives as living proofs.

"He teaches my hands to war;" Psalms 144:1. The craving of man is for the supernatural. This craving he has carried into almost everything he does including his thoughts and interests. Most A-list movies are movies that represent some supernatural ability. Imagine how men yearn and crave for the supernatural knowingly or unknowingly! King David explains that the secret of his extraordinary victories and conquests is that the Lord "teaches" him how to fight. God is his trainer! But whoever saw the Lord teaching him? No one! And obviously he was victorious in his battles. This means that his saying God teaches him, isn't no vain claim. This divine mentoring must have been a personal, spiritual experience that metamorphosed David into a champion without going through any physical tutoring. Like we see in the movies, people with supernatural abilities always defeat their merely physical counterparts. To be extraordinarily successful, garner the spiritual secret.

I once preached a sermon titled, "Understanding Jehovah as Your Strong Refuge". In that message, I didn't hesitate to stress that the most disadvantaged of people are people without a spiritual source or back up. Be it evil or good. For those who have Jehovah as their spiritual source, they are highly placed and cannot be compared to those who have a demonic source and more pitifully, those who don't belong anywhere.

In my assessment and disposition towards this book, owing to its practical nature, I think it can be referred to as a self-help book. And undoubtedly, every self-help book should carefully and honestly present its ideas. That's why although the contemporary society may seem to attach a whole lot of logic and may frown at spiritual or views they consider religious, I am presenting my ideas more from experience and practicality rather than logic and theory.

In my own experience, I look back and never cease to be amazed at my metamorphosis. I grew up being timid and shy. In my days in grade school (or primary school), I was unhealthily quiet. I was usually picked on by some of my mates. On one occasion, I contracted my elder brother Prosper, to help beat up one of the kid who was a torn in my flesh. He instead, asked me to beat up the kid or he would beat me up. I was perplexed. I was afraid of this kid; now, my brother also. So, I made my pick. I knew the boy was no match for him, so I decided to fight the boy knowing that in the event where the boy begins to beat me up; he would still come to my rescue. However, something astonishing happened. In fear of being beaten by my brother before the kid, I started beating the boy and he couldn't hit me even once. It is one of the most remarkable and funny events of my childhood. I told this story to give you a background of who I was before my encounter with this Secret 'P'. I am not Mike Tyson now; and I'm not chicken hearted either. But you get what I'm saying, right? I could not speak in the public. But I was occasionally picked among the kids who would make the class Bible recitation or presentation, no matter how shy I was. I was picked partly because the school knew my dad was a preacher, so they felt it would be easy for me to make Bible recitations. Suddenly, everything was about to change. Some things changed radically, others followed a steady process. I had encountered Him!

I never saw flames of fire in my room (or our room). I didn't hear a loud voice like thunder vibrate through the walls. I only saw positive changes in me, which I couldn't account for. Although, when I was much younger I used to have some mental visualizations that later would make me fear. I could not really explain it. But when I was 14, I had another strange experience (remember what I said earlier, "The Presence of God cannot be fully expressed but it is only best experienced"). So, I won't go into details that may not really matter because of the variations in individual experiences with God. However, it was this encounter that further thrust me into this secret 'P' — His Presence. God was more interested in me than I could ever be in Him. But also, my desire to know was not unnoticed. At this point I started having more matured experiences, getting unnatural answers. Beautiful experiences! Some of those experiences were not pleasurable but they fulfilled their purpose; to keep me always abiding. I was now more accepted, sometimes irrationally rejected. I began to climb the heights of spiritual glory and bliss. I also on some occasions fell into the valleys of spiritual despondency. However, one thing was now obvious; I had got His consciousness which I could not silence. It convicts me of sin, pricks me to repentance, pushes me to restitute and repent but more importantly has given me a personality that will make failure impossible.

How accessible is this presence, can anyone come in, how, is there anything to be done? When I was about 15 years old, I listened to my Dad read Psalm 15. It is a beautiful scripture. It left me pondering on the question of David in the early verses. I felt within me that owing to the nature of man, no one was really worthy to abide in the LORD's Presence. In fact, I thought David used the figure of speech where a question is asked, and an answer is not really anticipated. But that didn't put an end to my wondering over that scripture. I further looked at the succeeding verses. I saw the qualities of those who could abide. I was entrapped by one statement, "And speaks the truth in his heart…" Psalms 15:2.

I grew up with so much appreciation of honesty. My mother would always tell us that when we lie, we may think there is no eye witness, so we can easily get away with it, but God sees us. I didn't want to be enemies with God. I had this strong apprehension for God. I felt mean and bad things would always happen to enemies of God. I knew I couldn't hide from him either because my mom would always tell us that He sees everything even in the dark. So, I resolved to tell the truth to people especially my parents whenever I am asked about anything. However, I didn't really know about speaking the truth to myself. I seldom told myself the truth. I would later realize that to speak the truth to myself is to be unbiased in analyzing myself and my actions and accept the truth of whatsoever action I must have taken and repent following the pricking of my conscience. I didn't need to wait for someone else to tell me I have wronged before I would know that I have done wrong. I desperately wanted to dwell in the presence of the LORD, so I asked Him for Grace to be honest with Him and to myself. I resolved to tow the path of honesty inside-out. It wasn't so easy and has not been. (I have lost a lot of things and have made right a lot of things, when I weigh them on the new balance of my life –Honesty inside out.) If this was the requirement, I was willing to pay the price that would make me never the same.

Every relationship is established on the foundations of honesty. Without honesty there can be no intimacy. Your ability to honestly relate your fears, weaknesses, doubts etc is what will bring you into this reflective relationship with the Lord. In the Bible, King Solomon honestly told the Lord of his apparent inadequacy to lead the people of Israel following his father's demise and coronation as King. He tells the Lord of his immaturity and inexperience. His honest approach saw him obtain favor before the Lord, to ask whatsoever he may. He asks the Lord for wisdom; not only did he get wisdom, God also gave him a fame and name unlike any other King before or after him. If we are honest in our relationships even our spiritual relationship, we relate without fear or pretense. This goes a long way to establish the spiritual presence over us.

Perhaps one of the dreadful things about success, physical success, is the bane that comes with it. Many people become vulnerable and feel the lonely space in their hearts broadened upon achieving success. Because success most times turns you into a spectacle of admiration more than concern and care. People tend to have this unrealistic imagination of strength and power of the successful. Their loneliness and needs go unrecognized. Other times friends and family imagine that they have all the people they need to keep them company. This is the bane of success, which makes the successful sometimes want to wish otherwise. Imagine success without loneliness. Imagine a sweet gentle presence that breeds confidence and comfort. Imagine a presence that brings answers, natural and unnatural. The presence of The Lord satisfies you. An attempt to impress people, to be accepted by them or try to prove a point is only a reflection of an underlying insecurity which can be truly satisfied and filled by the presence of The Lord. You don't need to be an alien to have this sort of experiences you can experience it whoever you may be.

Most times people question the reality of Christ and His message.

To them, they may only believe by reason of a logical explanation. Well, this may continue to be difficult for them because unlike our human, physical world where "seeing is believing", in the spiritual realm, you believe then you see. Jesus Christ laid claims to a verifiable experience in scripture. He said, "Behold, I stand at the door and knock. If anyone hears my voice and opens the door, I will come in to him and dine with him and he with Me10" Usually, I will tell people, "Why don't you ask Him in? Experience Him and if you honestly do all He asks you to do, and you don't make out a reasonable positive observation, you could ask Him out". If anyone honestly seeks for the LORD, He'll satisfy totally. Some people may think this is only a fanatical statement. Well, for anyone who has had an experience with Him and for some careless reason lose touch with Him, they know it is not. Because when the presence leaves you, you lose touch with yourself, your environment and even life in general. Things no longer make meaning to you. This is a very depressing state to be in.

Life is more spiritual than physical. What you see sterns from what you cannot see. So, in reality, it is not what you see that matters, but what you cannot see. If success was by physical labor alone, those who are really successful may not be holding the status they enjoy. The real difference lies in the spiritual influence. There is a future we cannot see; events and fate we cannot decide; factors which may not always work out as planned. These things don't all go by physical explanations. While some people could be victimized by events and happenings, others are favored by them. The champions are fully aware of the spiritual side to life. Entrust an uncertain future into the hands of a certain God.

ABOUT THE AUTHOR

Favor E. Alanwoko is an author and teacher. He holds a Bachelor of Arts degree in History and International Studies, from Imo State University, Owerri. He is a member of All Nations International Ministers Fellowship in Prescott Valley, Arizona. His dynamic, insightful and exciting teaching approach distinguishes him greatly among other things. He lives in West Africa, Nigeria with his family.

email: thepreacher2day@yahoo.com

www.ingramcontent.com/pod-product-compliance
Lightning Source LLC
Chambersburg PA
CBHW050603300426
44112CB00013B/2057